SOLACE

Allagash Tails Vol. VI

Tales from

A National Wild and Scenic River

Written by: Tim Caverly

Illustrated by: Franklin Manzo Jr.

Edited by:

Copy editor/Proofreader

Nancy's Proofreading, Lewiston, Maine

njsm@roadrunner.com

Foreword by: Bob Duchesne

CONTENTS

AFTERWORD

GOLDEN RETRIEVER AWARD

FOREWORD

It seems like I've known Tim Caverly forever, though we've only been personal friends for a couple of years. It happens that we have been treading the same ground for over three decades. His 32 years as a ranger in the Maine Department of Conservation, most of those years as superintendent of the Allagash Wilderness Waterway, coincide with my love affair with the north Maine woods. In fact, my wife and I honeymooned on Chamberlain Lake in 1978. Reading one of Tim's stories is as relaxing as paddling downstream with a tailwind.

Tim anchors his tales to the Maine wilderness like a fire tower bolted to a granite mountaintop, steadfast and unmovable. The sagas may be fictional, but the setting is unerringly real to the last detail. It is the strength of Tim's writing that he sees no need to create an imaginary place when the real thing cannot be improved upon. Every location, every feature, every historical reference can be found on the Maine map. Nonresidents may not realize that the fictional accounts are painted on a genuine tapestry, but native Mainers smile at each geographical and cultural reference. We know these places, and we love them.

The people are real, too. Every rural Mainer knows George, whom you will meet in these pages. There is a George in every township. The Maine forest is not a lawless place, but application of the rules tends toward the pragmatic. There is tolerance for characters who color a little outside the lines. It's been like that for hundreds of years.

Every Allagash Tail is also rooted in a strong sense of family, spanning generations. This allows the author to jump around a bit in time and space without losing the reader. Woodcraft in the Maine forest is a skill not usefully learned from textbooks. It is a rough country awareness handed down from parents, elders, and mentors, tying generations together. As the world becomes increasingly complex, the forest remains a refuge of simplicity. Fire building is a constant necessity. Reading the weather in the clouds of a sunset is a survival skill. Paddling is an art.

Northern Maine is God's Country. So it is perfectly natural that there be a little bit of the supernatural in every Allagash Tail spun by Tim Caverly. Tim has the knack of spicing up his stories with otherworldly color without threat of malevolence. It works.

God's Country steals souls. Nobody who experiences the Allagash Wilderness Waterway or Baxter State Park remains unmoved. For he who tries his hand at living in the woods, even for a little while, the pull of nature is strong. He will return, again and again. Some will stay. Just as nature gripped Tim Caverly as a young boy, his accounts of outdoor life in the north woods grip the reader. Turn the page and prepare to be gripped.

Bob Duchesne

January 2015

As a young boy, Bob Duchesne spent too much time in the woods, plunking cans with a BB gun when he should have been raking leaves around his family's sporting camps. Bob is a graduate of Colby College in Waterville, Maine, and that is the city where he accidentally began a 42-year career in radio. However, a passion for birding preceded radio, and he's been enthralled by birds ever since first grade when goldfinches would sit on his lawn after school, adorning the green grass with the yellowest of yellow. As his radio career wound down, Bob established the Maine Birding Trail and now guides professionally, often up into the headwaters of the Allagash.

DEDICATION
"TO MY DAD"

Irvin C. Caverly Sr. and sons

at their Cornville home (T. Caverly collection).

"You're just like your father," the irritated camper stammered at me. Obviously upset, the man was mad because I had—once again—caught him in the act of violating state regulations. Frustrated at being found, the violator had thrown what he considered to be the ultimate insult. This wasn't the first time the man had been caught by members of my family.

I had first learned about the lawbreaker and his habit of doing whatever he pleased the day I was appointed to the position of waterway supervisor. At the time, the Director of the Bureau of Parks told me about this person who had spent years ignoring one state law after another. One of my first assignments as ranger-supervisor was "to watch the man and straightened him out."

So on the day I caught the guy committing numerous violations; I informed the man that if his actions didn't cease, he would be going to court, for each and every violation. The fellow became very angry when he realized I was canceling his plans for the day. His fury had been fueled further when he realized that I was the son of a forest warden who had caught him in similar acts years before.

While canoeing upstream after dealing with the dubious

character, I thought about his comment, and about my dad.

My father, Irvin Christopher Caverly, Jr. was a tall, gentle man, and even after having three sons and a life full of challenges, to my knowledge, never cursed. In fact, the strongest language I ever heard him use was "Oh poppycock," an old fashioned British term for "Oh baloney."

My Dad was born in Massachusetts, the son of Irvin C. Caverly, Sr. of Somerville, Massachusetts and Edda Locke Caverly of Cornville, Maine. Remembering, I realized that my father's life challenges begun at an early age. When my father was just eight years old, his mother became so sick that his father was forced to admit Edda into a Bangor hospital; an institution where my dad's mom would remain for the rest of her life.

Since my father didn't have a mum at home, he was "farmed out" to live with an aunt where he attended a school in Cornville. While my dad lived in Maine, his father remained living in Somerville, Massachusetts, where he sold and repaired automobiles.

Eventually dad married my mother Pauline Stevens, a Cornville native. During their first years of matrimony my father needed to build a home for his family. To save money, he decided to move a small building from his deceased mother's property, across a field and through the woods to a vacant lot near Route 150. Physically skidding, pushing, and rolling the inherited building a few feet at a time, Irvin eventually settled the structure onto the new foundation, a mile away from where he started. Within a few days, a local carpenter who was helping with the interior construction of Irvin and Polly's new home, accidentally spilled hot coals onto a pile of shavings and burnt my parents' house to the ground.

After the loss of the dwelling, the family misfortune continued. In 1942, four years after my brother Buzz was born, my mother delivered a third child; who they named James Lewis. In November of that year– just a few months old–the infant developed an incurable illness and died.

Shortly after the death of James, my father received word that his dad was very ill. Dad rushed the 200 plus miles from Cornville to Somerville to see his father [Irvin Sr.] "in time" only to learn upon his arrival that his father had already passed. In one year, and by age 29, my father had lost both his dad and a son.

Several years later my father experienced another death in the family. When my mom's dad needed nursing care, they brought him to our Cornville home where they cared for Gramps until he died.

My father's challenges continued and even getting to work wasn't easy. Employed to cover the night shift at a Skowhegan woolen mill, my dad couldn't afford a car. After supper he would hug his boys' goodnight and then walk the 5 miles to begin his daily job as a floor supervisor. After his 10 hour shift of walking throughout the plant, Dad would then hike the long ways back home and to his day job of farming and raising a family.

Rising early each morning Dad would tend crops on an 80-acre farm, and when he wasn't milking cows, fixing fence posts, or doing other countless chores around the farm, he'd find time for his sons.

In the late 1950s Dad learned that the mill was closing and that he would have to seek other employment. Eventually, he applied for and was appointed to a position with the Maine Forest Service. With this job he promised to protect property and our State's wild lands from fire. The work became a job he treasured; but accepting the warden's job also brought sadness.

Working for the state meant that my Dad was required

to accept assignments throughout Maine, so now my mom and dad would have to leave the farm they loved. Driving down a dusty road with a wife, three sons and a collie dog; my Dad left behind a homestead which had been passed down from his mom and dad–behind.

For several years, everything went well in our family. Each of the boys developed individual careers and begin their own families; and my Dad became a grandfather. Brother Steve joined the Army and serve in hot spots all over the world. Buzz and Tim got their own appointments as Conservation officers. Most years we were even able to spend the holidays together where my Mom would prepare a full meal in, what seemed to be, only minutes.

However during my father's golden years once again he was faced with a hard decision. My Mom developed Alzheimer's. Dad kept my mother home as long as he could, but then the time came that she needed more care that he could provide so my mother had to be placed in a health care facility. Every day Dad would drive the 25 miles to her bedside with the families portable CD player, so the couple could listen to the music they had once loved—together. When Dad wasn't with Mom, he would be seeking opportunities to be with "his boys."

Even with all of his misfortune, I remember my father as being a very positive person with a desire to keep his family close. Even during the harshest of times, I don't remember him uttering an unkind word about anyone or complaining about what should have been. He had a great sense of humor, was a good singer, loved to write poetry, tell jokes, and overall I recall him as someone who looked forward to tomorrow.

And so to that person who so many years ago told me that "I was just like my Dad," all I can reply is "Thank you!"

Sincerely,

Tim Caverly

Millinocket, Maine

March, 2015

ALLAGASH LAKE

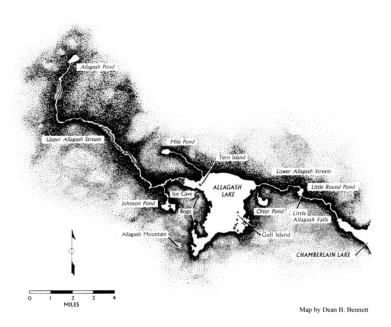

Map by Dean B. Bennett

PREFACE

The category or genre of this literary composition should, I suppose, be considered outdoor mystery fiction, and that may be the case. However, if the reader studies the pages closely they will find hints of autobiography, historical nonfiction, historical fiction, science fiction, realism, and prose; all topped off with a slice of life. The reason for such diversity is because many of the incidents discussed are based on my 32 years as a ranger with the Maine Park Service.

While a sundry of events did occur, the majority of individuals that I describe did not or do not exist. If a reader finds any similarities to themselves or to another it is purely a coincidence and was not my intent. For example, in the text the reader will read reports by correspondent Tim Holt, a reporter for the newspaper Forest Frenzy. Mr. Holt is an imaginary character, as is the newspaper; neither one is genuine.

Then again, a few of the characters either were or are real. For example, the piece titled "How Smart Are Beavers?" did appear as written many years ago in the Waterbury (Connecticut) Republic Newspaper. The main character, Bert Dumas, was my wife's grandfather who lived at the foot of Millinocket Lake.

Other individuals mentioned are also based on actual people, such as my portrait of Ulysses Grant (Lester) Stevens. Lester was my grandfather who had a farm on Hilton Hill in Cornville, Maine.

In these pages you will also find a picture and mention of a Lt. Joseph Sanborn. I do not know a lot about Joseph other than he is a distant relative (on my great-grandmother's side of the family) and that he fought for the Union army during the Civil War. The lucky coin that is mentioned in the story does exist—I have it framed along with Mr. Sanborn's picture—and the penny is engraved JCS, which we believed to be Joseph's full initials. The rest of the information about Joseph, such as his activity during the war of the rebellion, obituary, etc. is fiction and should be treated as such.

The geographical sites that I mention such as Rogue Bluffs State Park, Jasper Beach, the University of Maine at Machias, the town of Cornville, and Allagash Lake are real and each one a Maine treasure.

So it is up to you, the reader, to use your detective skills to determine what parts of the following text is fiction or nonfiction, autobiography or a fabrication, historic narrative or creative writing. Let me know what you decide.

Sincerely,

Tim Caverly

Millinocket, Maine

March, 2015

PART I

My mom told me that if I listen closely, with my ear near the edge, I will hear the river speak to me.

She said it will inform me of old mysteries, that it will encourage me to focus. My mom told me that the river knows everything and that if I am calm I will hear it wherever I am.

Abenaki Saying
Author Unknown

CHAPTER I

It's been a hell of a year and you could spell hell with a capital H for all I care! The young man grumbled quietly as he wiped away the inch-thick dust from the lid of an old steamer trunk. Sitting on his knees, the man bent over the grimy surface of the luggage and with calloused hands, brushed off dirt that had accumulated from years of neglect. The more of the powdery residue that was removed the more the sturdiness of the luggage was revealed; eventually revealing a shiny, black surface which shone under the dim light that seeped through a nearby attic window.

Once the dirt was removed, the man found the flat-top rectangular box to be of good size. Jim estimated the whole chest to be about 30 inches long, 16 inches wide, and must have been at least 12 inches deep. The corners were reinforced with decorative solid brass braces, and every seam was pinned by brass rivets placed an inch apart. So fortified, it was plain the container had been made to withstand hard travel. Then there was the cover of the trunk—*rugged enough to stand on*—Jim thought. Two and a half inch-wide by six-inch-long brass hinges held the large lid in place. The top was made even more secure by a brass latch and clasp riveted to the outer edge of the lip of the container. Snapped into the hasp was a heavily tarnished brass padlock that obviously hadn't been opened for quite some time. The lock was still solid in appearance and the man believed that *with a good polish the metal should clean up nicely.*

Stamped in the top of the piece of luggage was the manufacturer logo certifying the chest had been made in 1925 by the *Seward Trunk Company*. Centered over and just above the manufacturer's name, the monogram **JPC** had been pressed into the leather cover. Jim recognized the initials as belonging to his grandfather. Someone he'd never met, but who he had been named after.

Built to be hand carried, the container had three stitched, rawhide handles placed appropriately to aid with the ease of hauling. The first holder was centered on the front of the chest with the others placed on each end. The leather grips showed signs that they might have been coal black at one time, but now had become so dried by age that they displayed brown spider web like cracks throughout.

Three-inch wide metal bands circled lengthwise around the case which served as both trim and support. One strip was around the top, another around the bottom, and the third strap bound the shell in the middle; all served as an exoskeleton, providing an outer foundation to keep whatever that was inside–safe.

The man pulled gently on the front handle of the chest, and the luggage slid easily over the accumulated dirt and across the planked floor; away from the sloped roof where it had been stored. Once the trunk was fully exposed in the dusty sunlight filtering through the building's west, top-story window, he noted that the padlock was fastened tight.

Spying a can of WD-40 on a nearby shelf, Jim sprayed the shank of the lock and offered the lubricant into the keyhole. Jim gave the oil time to penetrate the tumblers of the security device while he dug for a key that he'd discovered in his father's safety deposit box.

Jim had been so busy with the farm that it had taken him sometime to retrieve the black metal "strongbox" from the bank in order to finally "close out" his parents' accounts. Leaving the bank with cash box in hand, Jim had returned home and placed the container on the kitchen table and reviewed the inherited effects. In the metal box Jim had found various antique coins, pictures of family treasures–taken for insurances purposes, birth certificates and then he'd seen the key. The only one in the container the key was small, gold colored and was attached by a cotton string to a label which identified that the key fit "the lock on the trunk." Finding the key–Jim sought out the family trunk which had been stored, unopened in the attic of the homestead for as long as he could remember.

Waiting for the oil to work Jim searched for the key that *he'd surely remembered to place* in one the four pockets of his pants.

To his right a full-length mirror appraised the man's appearance. Waiting for the oil to do its job, he stood straight; lit a cigarette, and studied the stranger who returned his gaze. Jim had always taken pride in his appearance, but he didn't care for the person he saw now. Through a dusty-covered reflection he could see the man in the mirror appeared older than his current age of 23. Once tall at six feet, two inches, the man's shoulders were now stooped from the burdens he'd carried for what seemed like forever. The likeness in the glass showed someone who hadn't shaved for at least two days; *nor had he bathed either,* he thought.

Long, brown hair flowed from under a frayed ball cap that had been worn for too long. Beneath the two-day-old growth of beard, a puffy face proved that the reflection hadn't bothered with proper eating habits or much physical exercise. His once white t-shirt was now dirty brown and sported a ragged tear about the size of a russet potato, just above his belly button. Through this rip, even a casual observer could see the white skin of a flabby stomach. The man's sagging paunch rolled over a two-inch-wide, black leather belt, further evidence that the person was heavier than he should be.

A thin wallet rested comfortably in a right back pocket of the pants secured by a long chain looped onto the belt of his pants. The tongue of the leather strap was secured to the buckle in the last hole available. His grease-covered jeans appeared to have been slept in, and the denims were begging for a good scrubbing. On his feet he wore a pair of work boots that wouldn't recognize a bottle of boot polish; even if the footwear had ever had the chance to be buffed.

Extinguishing the glow of the cigarette between his fingers and securing the butt in the left hip pocket of his pants, the man thought *if nothing else, I can at least make sure I don't set the old homestead on fire.* Ignoring the image, Jim returned to the task at hand. He placed the key into the keyhole, turned it to the right, and heard the quick snap of the lock as it allowed access to the box. Opening the lid of the family storage chest—

memories from the last three years climbed their way out of the deep recesses of his mind.

CHAPTER II

"Yes sir," the 21-year-old man said as he stood to follow the professor's instructions and introduce himself to the class. Standing in front of the others the young man thought guess the teacher doesn't know I hate speaking in front of a crowd. Timidly he stared over the heads of the others, at the wall along the back of the room, to avoiding making eye contact with his fellow students. The man cleared the nervousness from his throat and began.

"Ahem … ahemmmmm, my, my name is James Paul Clark and I'm from a small town outside of Skowhegan called Cornville." His speech was interrupted by the snickering classmates when they heard he was from such a hick-sounding settlement.

Standing red faced in front of the room, this was the undergraduate's first day of speech class where he was to be trained in the "fine art of verbal communication." Attending the University of Maine at Machias or UMM, the student cleared his throat and continued. "Hem, you can call me Jim and …" here the speaker was interrupted by an even louder laugh coming from the other 24 pupils waiting their turn to stand in front of the group. "You can call me Jim and I'm here at college so that I can …," his first speech was suddenly cut short by a loud bell that announced the end of class. While he watched, the whole student body rushed from the classroom in a hurry to get to the next instructor, who was famous for handing out early assignments and never offering to repeat his instructions.

"Teach others about the importance of our wild lands." Jim finished as he looked about the now-empty room. While the professor, Mr. Moody, stuffed papers into a faded brown briefcase, the teacher dismissed the young man with, "That was fine, Jim. You'll do well after you've presented a few speeches to the class."

"How many do I have to do?" Jim asked, hoping for the best. "Two or three?"

"Oh no, this is the first class of the term. You'll need to do a 20-minute speech once a week for the next eight weeks."

Nodding and replying ok to the instructor he thought drat, eight speeches. I'll never make it. Jim walked out of the room and stood in the lobby of Torry Hall. There Jim saw a fellow student bent over, getting a drink from the college's water fountain. To the young man's right, the entrance of the Merrill Library beckoned the nervous student and offered a fortress of solitude. *But no, he had another class to go to.* Thinking that a drink of cold water sounded like the right medicine to calm his red face, he waited for the scholar in front of him to finish.

While waiting, Jim stared at the official class schedule to determine the room assignment of the next lecture. The student at the fountain turned to face him. Jim saw the movement and looked up, directly into the deepest hazel green eyes he'd ever seen. *Heck, they aren't eyes; they are more like reflective pools of water staring right into my soul.* Gaping the young man froze in place mesmerized by a girl's dazzling white smile, coal black hair and a face that was tanned a radiant bronze. Intent on her facial features, Jim didn't even notice that the girl was wearing a sharp white blouse and green plaid skirt and black shoes. But it was the eyes—her hypnotic eyes that immobilized him. Freezing in place he thought *she is like a painting, yes-sir-re, I've stumbled onto a real-life Mona Lisa.*

Sensing that the young man was timid the girl spoke. "Hi, my name is Susan." Continuing, she explained, "I was in the last class when you spoke."

"Oh gosh, I hope I wasn't too embarrassing with

everyone laughing and all."

"They weren't laughing at you, you know." Susan explained. "It's just that everyone knew their turn was coming and they were feeling your nervousness."

While Jim unconsciously stared at this girl in front of him, Susan appraised the young man whom she'd noticed the minute he had walked into the room. Standing about six inches taller than the girl, the gent had moved easily, and walked with a quiet confidence toward his seat to wait for the professor to begin. She noticed his light brown hair, white teeth, and muscular frame. A slight grin indicated he was ready to laugh at a moment's notice and good humor sparkled in his eyes. And through his presentation, even though he was nervous, Susan could tell that with a little practice he would be very good at public speaking.

Jim's clothes were not new, but they were clean, well patched, and clung to a muscular frame. *Yes*, she thought, *maybe, just maybe here was the* … and here Susan decided to let her thoughts drift off.

Jim asked, "Which way are you headed? I can walk a ways if you want?"

Susan smiled, and nodded ok, and turned towards a

classroom located at the south end of the building. Walking beside the young man and beyond the entrance to the student lounge, the girl's left arm lightly brushed this tall man's right sleeve; the young woman thought she could hear music in the air.

CHAPTER III

Soon the two individuals became an actual twosome. Memorizing each other's class schedule, the man and woman would find excuses to seek out the other. First it was to get a study assignment, borrow a class handout, or to copy notes. Often Jim would time his work-study assignment of rolling ace bandages for the athletic department, so he'd be in the training room whenever Susan passed by, on her way to physial education.

Susan knew the times when Jim ate his meals at the Commons and would take her food at the same time. Always coming up behind her friend to shyly inquire, "Is the seat beside you taken, I have a question to ask?" The seat was always available and their conversation came so easily that Susan never did remember to ask her questions.

Eventually on weekends they would walk downtown along the historic main street to eat a piece of strawberry pie at Helen's Restaurant. A popular eatery located in the middle of the Shire town; the slabs of dessert were so huge that the two always shared. One Friday night the couple discovered the Colonial Theater and met the proprietor, a Mrs. Emma Means, who made sure that only "proper behavior" occurred in her theater. Their first real date occurred in the only playhouse in the college town. It involved watching a movie called T*he Son of Flubber*, a Walt Disney classic, about which Jim would later joke "I guess that flick defined the basis of our friendship."

The next show they shared was *Dr. Zhivago*, an epic film that they saw four times. It wasn't that the couple enjoyed the movie that much, but Jim liked the way Susan snuggled during the frozen winter scenes when the award-winning music of "Laura's Theme" filled the theater.

Then Jim bought a car. His father was sickly and the family thought it best for the student to have his own transportation. "They may not be able to drive to Machias much longer to bring him home to Cornville, for the holidays," his parents had explained.

It was blue, an almost deep blue 1995 Mercury Comet. Susan thought it was the prettiest car she had ever seen. Jim liked the way it handled and he could drive with one hand on the steering wheel and, by the way, the car had a very good radio. The transportation opened doors to new adventures.

Discovering Roque Bluffs State Park, the couple loved to visit the overlook at night and listen to music that flowed over the ocean from Boston radio stations. Streaming out of the car's speakers like a sweet fog, the classic song "Temptation Eyes" by The Grass Roots harmonized with the splashing waves that rolled in over the sand beach. A summer breeze carried the fragrance of wild roses from the nearby dunes through the open windows of the car.

A WILD ROSE WITH A FRIEND AT ROQUE BLUFFS STATE PARK, ROQUE BLUFFS, MAINE (T. CAVERLY PHOTO.)

Then there was Jasper Beach. Located in remote Bucks Harbor the rocky shore was a discovery that took their breath away. The 800-meter gravel beach composed of fine-grained red volcanic rock was reported to polish bright enough that the stone would gleamed in the morning light. Strolling along a beach of colored pebbles didn't make for easy walking, but the surges of tide choreographed a constant clicky-clack, clicky-clack, clicky-clack as the ocean's salt waves moved the stones back and forth. These were good years for the two who somehow, without planning, had become a couple.

JASPER BEACH, MAINE (T. CAVERLY PHOTO.)

And they had laughed; laughed a lot actually. One evening Jim had even tried singing to Susan. Not known as one who could carry a tune in a bucket, Jim had grown tired of cramming for the big test scheduled for the next day. So he decided to walk over to see what Susan was up to. It was after curfew and he knew better than to try the front door, and so Jim walked to the back of the girls' dorm.

Looking up, Jim saw that the light in Susan's room was still on. Throwing a pebble at the windowpane to get her attention, the girl opened the window and scolded him for coming over so late. Inside ... her heart leaped whenever she saw him. His being around always helped her feel better.

"What do you want, Mister Clark?" Susan questioned with good humor.

"I'm tired of studying and so thought I drop by to say hi."

"Well—hi." Smiled the girl.

"Have you ever heard me sing?" Jim asked.

"Yes," said Susan, "but please don ..." And before she could finish Jim broke out in a stanza of his favorite song "Jambalaya" written and sung by the famous country artist, Hank Williams. Absorbed in the music and singing with his eyes closed, he didn't even see Susan's roommate join her at the window. The two females whispered to each other, smiled and suddenly disappeared. "… Son of a gun we'll have big fun on the…," but Jim never got the chance to finish. As quick as scat, the girls returned with a pail of water and lifted it up to the windowsill. Once in place, Susan and her roommate each grabbed a side of the bucket bail and threw the water as hard as they could at the forlorn-sounding singer below. The splash hit Jim straight on, drenching the soloist, drowning out his music.

Deciding to call it a night after such a soaking, Jim walked away. Susan watched Jim slowly stroll back towards the men's dorm. She left the window open and heard his footsteps echo across the parking lot and smiled when she understood that he was now singing another Williams classic—"How can I free your doubtful mind and melt your Cold, Cold Heart." Climbing into bed she thought, *tomorrow I'll buy him a piece of pie at Helen's to make up for our trick.* She quickly went to sleep and dreamt of woodlands to explore with Jim.

Sharing plans for the future, they discovered a mutual interest in the Maine outdoors. As a young girl Susan had been sickly, but then she discovered Girl Scouts and Camp Natarswi. The legendary camp lay along the shores of Lower Togue Pond, and was handily located near the southern entrance of Baxter State Park. At camp she learned outdoor skills in camping, cooking, how to handle a canoe, and grew strong from hiking around and over mile-high Mt. Katahdin. While Susan had been at the camp, Jim had been in the park as well. He had a great-uncle who had worked for years as a ranger in the park and as a young man Jim had gone there to hike trails that his family had trek for years. In addition to the hiking, there had also been exploring ponds such as Grassy, Kidney, Daicey, and Rocky; where Jim loved to cast artificial flies such as the orange-bodied grasshopper, maple syrup, and the white miller.

Between classes, the two friends compiled a list of hikes and canoe trips they wanted to take. On top of their list was the seven-mile hike into the park's Russell Pond Campground, and two miles beyond where they could stand under the cascading liquid of Green Falls near the shore of Wassataquoik Lake. Water from the falls flowed over moss-covered rock, and sprayed so cold, a person could only shower for a few minutes; even on the hottest summer day.

Then there was the Allagash; a national wild and scenic river that flowed like a vein through the heart of the Maine woods. Why the intrigue of just the name alone promised unimagined adventures. While the two talked of several explorations, the Allagash stuck in both of their minds.

It was April and one morning, before the start of class, the couple talked about June and how the end of the school year was drawing near. *Maybe during the summer vacation they could do some hikes or canoe. It was going to be a wonderful summer and then next fall would be the beginning of their senior year and after graduation they could. ...*

Then Jim received a message to report to the office of the Dean of Students.

CHAPTER IV

Excused from class, Jim walked by a campus pond, which only two years prior had been a swamp. The college had decided that clearing the wetland would make a good work study assignment so a college janitor had given Jim an axe, a buck saw and told the student to clear the alders and tamarack from the marsh. Once Jim had removed the undergrowth, the area had been dug into a freshwater pond, and become a home to local wildlife. Strolling over nearby manicured lawns Jim could hear the raspy call of the green-headed mallard that had claimed the pool for his own; walking on by, he hoped *maybe the school had a new work assignment, lord knows he sure could use the money to help pay on his college loan.*

Passing through the doors of Powers Hall and up the stairs, the secretary to the Dean looked up from her desk at Jim's approach. With a forced smile she said, "Come right in, Jim. The Doctor is expecting you." And without another word or glance she led the way to the administrator's office. Sitting behind a mahogany desk, covered with forms and two calculators; the professor was busily working on budgets trying to balance the numbers so the college wouldn't have to increase the cost of tuition. Concentrating so hard on the financial plan, the professor didn't see Jim at the door. "Damn it—the cost of doing business keeps going up. I hope we aren't going to have to threaten layoffs again this year. And if this isn't enough—I dread what I have to do next!"

Using the knuckles of his right hand Jim knocked softly on the open door of the Dean's office. Startled the professor looked up, and immediately recognized one of the hardest-working students that the university had ever employed.

"Come in Jim, come in. Can I get you a soda, coffee, or water? Oh and close the door will you? Have a seat, have a seat." The dean said without waiting for an answer about the offer of a hot or cold beverage.

Gosh he acts nervous; Jim thought. *I hope he is feeling ok.* "No I am all set, just had a soda with Susan, thanks anyway."

"God I hate these situations." The dean thought out loud.

"What situation is that, Dean? Is the college in bad financial shape again, sir? I hope the school won't have to raise our costs ... I'm not sure I could find any more money. I have some saved towards the fall semester and with my summer job and all—I should be able to afford to finish out my senior year," said Jim, hoping he could make the obviously distraught man feel a little better.

"No, no, it's nothing like that. The budget will be fine, but I got some bad news for you, Jim."

"If it is the cost of my work study I guess I can cut back on some of my hours but I need the money, because …"

"No, Jim!" and now came the words that the dean dreaded, "It's your dad. He's sick, Jim. Your mom called and he is very, very sick. She needs you to come home immediately." Speechless at the news Jim's face turned white. "But I thought the radiation was working. I thought he was getting out of the hospital in a few days. I thought ..." Here Jim paused in midsentence for just a moment and then continued softly, "he can't be sick; he's my dad."

"I am afraid it's true, son. You'll need to leave as soon as possible. I've asked your roommate to pack your belongings and put everything in your car."

"But how will I finish my classes, what about Susan?"

"Jim, listen to me! You need to leave right now! We'll worry about your classes later. If you go right now you might make it in time to …" Here the dean changed the topic and continued, "I'll explain to Susan; she is smart and she will understand."

Overcome by grief, Jim flew out of this dreaded office, that he now hated, and descended the 12-foot length of stairs in three leaps. Running Jim headed straight to the girls' dorm at Dorwood Hall and to Susan's room. *He'd find her and tell his friend the news; that he had to leave unexpectedly and why. Then he'd give Susan his phone number and when his dad was better they would see each other and talk.*

Running across campus, Jim sailed through the glass door of the girls' dorm. Running down a forbidden hallway he came to Susan's room on the building's first floor. He tried the doorknob but it wouldn't turn—it was locked. He pounded on the door calling her name, "Susan, Susan—I have to talk with you." But there wasn't any answer—she wasn't there.

Still breathing heavy from running, he moved at a slower pace towards his car and for the Redington Memorial Hospital in Skowhegan.

*****

Turning his car onto Route 1, the dean's words from a few minutes ago finally sunk in. *If you go right now you might make it in time to ...*

To! To what? The man worried. Then Jim pushed the accelerator of the little blue car to the floor. Whatever the dean meant, the son wanted to see his dad in time.

Driving west on the paved highway, he flew by the blueberry barrens and didn't even see the farmers preparing the field. Pushing over a bridge and through the town of Cherryfield, he never noticed the blue coolness of the Narraguagus River. Jim didn't even know he had driven through the Black Woods on Route 182 until he pulled up to the red stoplight in Ellsworth. When the light turned green he headed north on Route 1A. He'd stay on that highway until he got to Bangor. Once in the Queen City he'd take I395 to I95. Jim would then follow the Interstate to Newport. From there he'd turn onto Route 2 and finish the final twenty miles to Skowhegan and to his dad and mom. Fighting back his tears, he thought about his parents.

CHAPTER V

The student and his parents had always been very close. James Paul or Jim, as he was usually called, was the couple's only son and had been named after a grandfather. Jim had heard that his parents tried to have children for years, only to be repeatedly disappointed; finally the husband and wife decided to adopt.

Running the gambit of the adoption process for over a year, the pair finally received word that they were next on the list to receive a child—which they could expect to take delivery of in about 12 months. Three months after receiving word about adoption, the wife announced she was pregnant. The couple no longer needed to seek out a child; one of their own was on the way.

The couple was pleased to bring their son home to their farm in Cornville. The 80-acre homestead didn't make them rich by any means, but it produced enough milk, beans, corn, hay, livestock and in the fall, apples; so that most months the family could meet their financial obligations. Then the wife would add income to their meager earnings by raising collies or by making wreaths to sell at the Congregational Church; and, from time to time, she would take in boarders. It wasn't a rich life, but if they were careful they could get by; and they were happy.

When Jim was old enough to walk on his own through the forest, his mom and dad would take him hunting and fishing; as often as they could get away from the farm. His father taught the boy how to be a woodsman; the proper way to carry an ax, how to build a campfire in the rain, the right way to use a compass, and the suitable way to build an outdoor shelter (just in case he ever got caught out overnight). At night Jim and his dad would sit outside on the front porch listening to peepers or watching the lightning from faraway storms— never going inside until complete darkness had set in.

Jim's mother was colorful and equally knowledgeable about the outdoors. "Heck," Jim's dad used to say; "Your mom could catch a brook trout in a mud puddle." Jim's mother had gone on her first fishing trip with her dad, Lester, when she was just four years old. The little girl had struggled to keep up and after a short distance her dad had picked up his daughter and placed her in his pack basket to lug the child on his back. Now that the girl didn't have to watch where she was going; the little one jabbered continually about the birds, the trees, the flowers, and at some point would point to the sky and ask,

"Daddy what does the shape of that cloud look like to you?" Arriving at a brook, Lester would remove a monofilament line and fishhook from his pocket, cut a sprig of alder and rig up a fishing pole for his little girl. And being a proper father, he always agreed that any trout that his daughter caught was of course, bigger than his.

As a young boy, Jim had been told about his mother's colorful behavior. One day Jim's dad had been feeding hay to the cows when he heard a rifle shot ring out from one of the upstairs windows of the farmhouse. Scurrying from the barn, the husband ran around the front of the home just in time to see Jim's mother pulling the barrel of her deer rifle; a Model 94, 38–40 Marlin carbine, back inside.

Leaning out of the second-story bedroom window, the wife hollered, "I just shot a porcupine that was going towards the dog's pen. Go bury that thing, will you?—before one of our dogs gets into it."

Jim remembered hearing that the family's love of the woods had originated from a great-grandfather who had served in the Civil War. But he didn't know much about whom, why, or how the early ancestor had learned about the north woods. When Jim pulled into the hospital's parking lot, the memories faded back into his mind. Jim shut off the ignition to the car and walked to the entrance of the care facility only to meet his mother coming out. Red-faced with swollen eyes, it was obvious the elderly lady had been crying for quite some time.

"Mom, how's dad?" the son asked; dreading the answer.

"Your father has passed, Jim. He tried to hold on, but he died about an hour ago. Your dad's body has gone to the funeral home."

"But I, I thought he was getting better?" Jim queried not wanting to believe the news.

"He did for a while. But he was too sick for too long and his heart couldn't take the strain of fighting the cancer. He told me to tell you that he loved you. Let's go home, son."

Silently the new widow and son climbed in the blue Comet and headed to the farm in Cornville.

*****

Several days later the family funeral was held in the Skowhegan Congregational Church. Some of the town's folks said it was the biggest memorial service they had ever seen.

Two days after the funeral there was the reading of the

father's will. Jim was stunned to learn that he had inherited the farm and that he would get the deed only if he promised to take care of his mother for the rest of her days.

Jim accepted the ownership and became a full-time farmer. There were crops to get in and bills to be paid. His father's illness had been very costly and their health insurance hadn't been very good. In trying to do it all, Jim didn't have time to think about returning to college or to call his friend Susan.

CHAPTER VI

For two years life on the farm seemed ok. By working before daylight to after dark seven days a week; Jim was able to keep up with most of the bills. But it was a very busy time in his life. Often the farmer would fall exhausted into bed at night, so tired that he didn't notice that his mother was starting to overlook things. At first it wasn't necessarily important items; just stuff like forgetting where she had put the newspaper or not being able to find her cookbook. But then her memory loss got real hazardous. She might leave the electric stove on for hours, neglect to close the door to the firebox of the wood stove, or forget that a person shouldn't put metal coffee cups in a microwave oven. Once she nearly set the place on fire when she walked away from bacon frying on the stove to watch TV. Jim had come through the door, just as a small flame was candling off the grease in the cast iron skillet.

Then the mom started pacing outside around the farm; always wanting to walk up hill. Jim's mother had been raised on the highest ground in the area, Hilton Hill. There her father, Ulysses Grant (aka Lester) Stevens had a farm. She would leave the house and walk up hill for hours. When asked where she was going, the elderly woman would tell her son that she was going home.

Finally, after an afternoon appointment the doctor confirmed Jim's worst fears. "I am sorry Jim, but your mom has Alzheimer's. And I am afraid it is in its late stages. She will need constant care—I suggest she be placed in the nursing home next to the hospital."

Jim stared without responding and so the doctor continued. "It is really best for you and for her safety. And she should be admitted as soon as possible."

The son had left his mom at the eldercare that day and kissed her a gentle good-bye on her forehead. That night Jim went home to a house so big and empty that his footsteps echoed as he walked from room to room.

The doctor's prognosis was correct and her disease progressed fast; in fact so rapidly that within six months the Clark family had a second family funeral.

Jim didn't smile much now and never left the farm unless it was to deliver goods to market. Then the tornado came. It was a storm so severe that it laid flat his crop of beans, corn, and hay, ruining months of work. The only thing left was the farm animals.

Pouring over an endless pile of bills Jim thought, *I'll*

never bring in enough income from milk, eggs, and beef to make my monthly payments. Guess I'll have to raise money by selling something. But what?

That night is when Jim started having the dreams.

CHAPTER VII

He is flying in a plane, a small, two-person Piper Cub. Jim can see the whole interior and that the craft has tandem seats. The pilot is sitting in the fore seat and Jim is sitting in the aft. Both are wearing radio headsets and seat belts. The navigator is constantly watching the gauges, scanning the skies for other aircraft, and pointing out objects of interest below to his passenger.

Jim is sitting directly behind the pilot and they are carrying on a conversation through their communication headsets. Jim can't see out the plane's windshield because the aviator's body blocks his view. Looking out the side window Jim can see the blue water, green softwood forest, and every once in a while the muddy line across a brook made by a startled moose in an attempt to escape the unwelcome the hum of the aircraft.

The pilot is continually talking about the logging history of the area on the ground below and points out local landmarks as they pass by. There are the grown–in–fields of a back woods settlement known as the Chamberlain Farm. Sitting high on the shore by the farm is the rusted remains of an abandoned work boat called the Marsh. The pilot continues speaking and says they are now approaching the Tramway where there are two discarded trains that were originally hauled into the woods in the 1920's and are now part of a designated national historic district.

The pilot points to the locomotives now abandoned and silent in the forest below. Flying over a deteriorated trestle, where Allagash Stream meets the inlet of Chamberlain Lake, Jim looks down at the impressive structure and appreciates the difficult work it must have been to construct a 1500-foot railroad bridge miles from anywhere. Leaving the trestle behind, the pilot indicates a well-known fishing hole on the southwest side of Allagash Stream. He says that the angling site was once called the Masterman's Pool, but now it is better known as the "Allagash Pool." The flier tells Jim that it isn't uncommon for folks who fish there to hook a 4½ lb. brookie. To Jim's right and southeast, the rays of an early morning sun bounce off Mt. Katahdin. It's is a calm day, with little side wind, and the plane's pontoons cut smoothly through the air. Jim can smell the light aroma of the plane's exhaust. It's not a pleasant smell, but it isn't making him airsick either. The plane is also used to instruct others how to fly so there is a joystick (or control) directly between Jim's feet. The stick follows the front joystick that the pilot is using to navigate. *Jim is very careful not to touch this steering mechanism.*

The pilot starts to tell about an old trapper's camp on Allagash Lake, when he groans. Hearing the noise in his headset Jim looks at his pilot. The flier's face has turned gray and the man moans a second time. He then loses consciousness and passes out—falling forward onto the navigation aid. Jim realizes that the flier is having a heart attack. The weight of the still body of the pilot pushes the steering forward, forcing the plane into a nose dive. Jim, sensing danger, reaches forward for the control yoke, but the seat belt holds him back.

Jim releases the restraint to reach out to the pilot and pull the nose of the plane up. Jim doesn't know how to fly, but he has got to do something. The man is too heavy and the cockpit is too small. Jim can't move him. The plane is dropping quickly and an angry forest is coming up fast. Jim realizes they are going to crash and he braces for the pain...

Waking up in a sea of sweat, it takes Jim a minute to understand where he is. Then he realizes that it is time to milk the cows and feed the chickens. He gets up, dons work clothes worn the day before and heads down the stairs, shaking the dream out of his thoughts and off his mind.

*****

Finishing the morning chores, Jim loads the rattletrap truck with milk for delivery to the dairy. Grabbing a cup of coffee at the local convenience store he sees a sale on unfiltered cigarettes. He buys his first pack ever and grabs a donut to go with the bitterly hot morning liquid.

CHAPTER VIII

Several nights later Jim has another dream.

It's winter and he's wearing some sort of uniform. He is standing on the shore of Round Pond in T6R11 when he sees the approach of a small yellow plane. The aircraft is equipped with skis rather than wheels. It is a Piper Cub and Jim knows the plane belongs to the State Fish and Game Department. He realizes that a game warden pilot is coming to pick him up.

Jim recognizes the pilot and he also knows that just last year the aviator had crashed his plane. The accident had happened during an attempt to land the state plane on the ice and snow of Moosehead Lake. The warden aviator was coming in slowly when an unexpected crosswind caught the aircraft and flipped it upside down. The pilot escapes the mishap with only bruises—the plane was a total wreck. The state has issued the flier another aircraft and he is coming to give Jim a ride.

The plane lands, taxies to a halt and Jim picks up his backpack off the snow and climbs into the back seat. In the pack is everything he will need if he gets caught out overnight: a space blanket, food rations, matches, hot coffee, compass, flashlight, dry mittens, two-way radio, small axe, and a first aid kit. The pilot takes off and they are flying over the trains on the way to check harvest operations on distant Allagash Lake; Jim keeps the pack on his lap.

After three hours in the air they return to Round Pond. The pilot approaches the ice-covered pond. They are 20 feet over the ice when the flier starts shouting "come on, come on, come on!" The plane refuses to respond to controls. The craft won't go up or down. Jim looks at the joystick between his feet. His pack has slipped off his lap, falling between the back of the pilot's seat and the navigation stick—jamming the control so the pilot can't steer.

The aircraft is flying directly towards a large pine—the pilot can't maneuver the plane—they are going to crash! Jim clasp his hands together behind his head—places his head between his knees with elbows pointing toward the floor of the plane and braces for the impact.

Jim wakes up before the crash. Shaking his head in disbelief that he is having "the airplane dream" again; he swings his feet over the edge of the bed and reaches for the cigarettes left on the nightstand.

It's dark and still no sign of dawn, but Jim decides to go to the barn anyway. Today he is selling the family's favorite Hereford, "Brickie." It's been a hard decision to sell an animal that had become a family pet. His dad bought the red bull as a baby and it was so smart and handsome that the whiteface had quickly become his favorite. Jim has grown up with the four-legged friend—it was the first thing he had responsibility for and the calf used to follow him around like a dog. But now Jim needs the money that the bull will bring.

CHAPTER IX

Returning to the farm after delivering Brickie, Jim turns off Route 150, up the dirt road towards the family homestead. The two-story farmhouse, built in the early 1800s sits at what was once a strategic business intersection of the Revere School Road and the Oxbow Road. In the early 19th century the colonial-style home had been a popular tavern when the street was the main highway from the Beckwith Road (now Route 150) to the West Ridge byway. Jim's dad inherited the farm from Jim's grandmother and took pride in the family heritage and the local history the homestead represented.

Hand-hewed beams fastened together by wooden pegs demonstrated that the home was solidly built. The house was painted classic white with Greek columns that supported a portico over the front porch. The farmhouse even had hidden shutters that could be closed over the windows, from the inside, in case of Indian attack.

Without Brickie, the farm seemed exceptionally quiet. Returning from the sale, Jim didn't go to the barn but entered the house, walked up the stairs, and passed by the door of his bedroom to a second set of treads. This flight of steps led to the top floor or attic of the house. On the fourth step Jim paused for just a moment to look at the secret compartment in the stairwell. Now empty, it was where his mother used to conceal sugar. The hiding place, accessed by a sliding tread, was built during World War II when the federal government had placed a limit on the amount of sugar that people could possess. Jim's grandfather, who lived nearby, had a much smaller family so he would always give his sugar allotment to his daughter–Jim's mother.

The extra sugar put Jim's family over the maximum allowed so; Jim's mom had kept the sweetener concealed in case the "sugar police" happened to stop by.

Continuing up the flight of stairs, Jim came out into the unfinished attic. In the place where boards were missing from planked over floor, an experienced observer could still see traces of dried corncobs that had once been packed between the stringers to serve as insulation against the cold winters. The building had stood for over 200 years and there wasn't any sign of weakening.

But now that his family was gone, it was time to inventory and remove some of his mother and dad's unneeded things.

Walking the length of the giant open room, the man

noticed that everything seemed covered in dust. Halfway down the room he saw a dark rectangular object tucked against the south wall; something that at first glance seemed to be some sort of coffer.

CHAPTER X

Even with the help of the WD-40, the hinges of the trunk squeaked in protest at having its top removed. If it could talk—the luggage would probably ask—where have you been? *I've been waiting too long; your granddad and I had some neat adventures.* But the chest couldn't talk, so Jim looked at the contents inside.

The interior of the chest was well appointed. The inside of the cover was lined with maroon-colored upholstery. The richness of the fabric was reinforced along the edges with a white oak trim.

The trunk had been used so much that in some places the fabric had been worn thin, which exposed the cedar lining underneath. The aromatic softwood was often used in luggage because of being lightweight and the resinous odor the wood emitted discouraged moths from chewing on the fabric.

The trunk was full. On top of a pile of clothes, Jim found a "Hunter's Photo Album and Log Book." Decked out in shapes of camouflage brown and green leaves, the scrapbook was full of pictures, diary entries, and newspaper articles about the Maine woods. Opening the cover, the first thing Jim saw was an old newspaper clipping and so he read:

How Smart are Beavers?

By Bert Dumas

Millinocket Lake, Maine

As told to Tom Egan, columnist for *The Sportsman's Corner*
Waterbury Sunday Republican, November 21, 1954

I had a cabin near a brook [in the shadow of Mt. Katahdin] that I used during the hunting and trapping season.

"I hadn't been there for a couple of months so I thought I would go see how things were. A colony of beavers had built a dam on the brook and flooded my cabin.

I had to wade through water up to my knees to get in the camp. I got a shovel and axe and made a hole in the dam and let the water out, as the camp was damp.

I left, but went back a few days later and noticed that the dam was repaired but there wasn't any water near the cabin. I went in and built a fire and noticed a lot of smoke. A piece of stovepipe was missing. I finally found it. The beavers had built it into their dam. They didn't want me to bother their dam again so they took the [section] of pipe with the damper in it and every time the water got up near the cabin they opened the damper.

BEAVER DAM (F. MANZO)

Smiling for the first time in months, Jim closed the cover and set the scrapbook aside to examine at a later date. Then he reached back into the trunk and began to remove the contents, one item at a time. He placed those items in a neat pile on the floor at his feet.

Under the album was a pile of old National Geographic magazines. Early on in life Jim had been told about the deep woods adventure called the Allagash; and that when the river corridor had first received State protection, there had been tons of periodicals published articles about the river's *wild character*. By the looks of the stack, it appeared that his grandfather had saved all of those National Geographic editions.

Beneath the magazines Jim found sporting equipment. There were fishing flies, a small hunting knife, compass, a stainless steel thermos, and bullets. The ammo, two boxes of 38–40 Winchester cartridges, which had a full complement of 50 shells in each carton. Wrapped around one of the boxes was an information sheet that explained that each bullet had 180 grains of lead and were center fire cartridges that was first introduced in 1864. Once fired, the shells would travel towards its target at 1,160 feet/second. Located on the cover of the box, in bold script, the Winchester Company proudly promised,

Any hunter using our ammunition is sure to bring home meat for the table.

The bullets intrigued Jim. He knew that his family

liked to hunt *I wonder if these shells are for the same gun my mom used years ago to shoot the porcupine. I haven't seen that gun in years. Wonder what ever happened to it?*

Placing the shells on top of the growing pile he started pulling out clothes. There were checkered shirts, wool pants, stockings, mittens, gloves, and caps. Union suits were shyly tucked under the trousers. Next he found a rain suit, cold weather parker, and two pairs of boots; a rubber pair for wet weather and leather footwear for hiking. A single hand-carved, black duck decoy leaned against the left side of the case. All of the contents had been packed in a state of readiness so when they were needed they could be removed in order of priority.

The chest was now empty and Jim began to repack the luggage. Putting the leather boots in first he accidentally dropped the right shoe into the container. The footwear bounced against the right side of the case, knocking free an envelope that had been taped against the interior's sidewall. Jim reached down to pick up the sealed letter which was yellowed with age. Pulling out the correspondence from its protected spot he was surprised to see shaky handwriting in the center of the document declaring:

To my Grandson on his 21st birthday

and in the upper left corner were scribbled the initials JPC.

Removing the correspondence, he closed the cover of the trunk. Jim stood, lit a cigarette, and turned to take a seat on the chest. Once in place, he unfolded the parchment pages, and saw several $100 bills fall to the floor. He picked up the money, held the uncounted currency in his left hand and read:

April 10, 1993

To my dear, dear grandson Jim,

I am writing from my hospital room to wish you a happy 21st birthday. My wishes are premature in that you haven't yet been born. As I write, your mom is expecting her first child and your parents have just been told they can expect a son to arrive around the first of June. Your mom was so excited that she immediately called to share their news.

After your parent's phone call, the doctor came to share the results of my recent biopsy. He says that my cancer has progressed faster than they thought and now my condition is terminal. The diagnosis is unclear if I will live a few weeks or a few months. Whichever it is, I hope I can be there when you are born. If we don't get a chance to meet, I pray your parents will tell you about me and the good times we shared.

If things go well, you will probably finish college in the spring of 2014 and I would love to be there. But I've had a good life and circumstances are what they are.

As with most people, I have made a few mistakes in life. I didn't exercise as much as I should and I often stayed too many hours at work. But I am proud to say that I've never intentionally hurt anybody, and that I don't owe a dollar to anyone. Maybe I didn't say it often enough, but I dearly love my family.

However, now that you're a man; I need you to do something. Several years ago I took a fishing vacation to Allagash Lake and camped at the Ice Cave campsite. While there a series of events occurred. First, just as I entered the lake, a gust of wind overturned a canoe traveling right in front of me as I entered the lake. Luckily I was close enough to pull the man, out before he got into real bad trouble. The person turned out to be an Allagash ranger on his way to a nearby camp.

Then a tornado blew through and that tempest was followed

by a torrential rain. It was blowing so hard that trees were falling throughout the campsite. Because of the storm the ranger was worried for my safety so he invited me to stay at his cabin. The weather got worse and a short visit turned into several days. The ranger's name is Dalton James. I found him to be an excellent woodsman and very knowledgeable.

During our hours of conversation he shared many tales about back woods lore and legend. After the storm, it was time for me to leave so I paddled up to Allagash Stream to Johnson Pond and back to my vehicle.

A few years later, after my last and final visit to the lake, I realized that I had left a family heirloom behind. Within three or four days of my departure Dalton called to tell me about the item I had left behind and he promised to keep it for me until I returned.

I always planned to go back, but time slipped away. Your parents were so busy that I didn't want to place any burden by asking them to retrieve it. But now I'd like you to contact Dalton as he may still have our property, or at least know where it is. The man will probably be retired from his ranger's job and most likely quite old. When you go to look him up please give Dalton this message. "Le moment est venu." He'll know what that means and my friend will tell you where my property may be found.

In the winter Dalton used to live in Millinocket, but can be found at his camp in the woods during the summer. The records clerk in the town office should be able to help you find him. For the sake of our family it is very important that you recover my heirloom!

Most of my savings have been used up by medical treatments, but I did manage to sell some of my hand-carved duck decoys. I've included that money with this letter as a graduation present and to help with the expenses of your trip to find DJ.

I am getting very tired so I'll end this letter with a poem I found in an old woods journal. I always like the thought-"In the forest is where man can heal his soul, and the curious mind will discover nature; yet untold."

Remember my boy, we all need special places where a person can restore physical and psychological health. I only hope that you will find your way to discover the outdoors, learn from Mother Nature's classroom, and regain our property.

I've asked your folks that upon my passing to spread some of my ashes in front of the Ice Cave Campsite on Allagash Lake. I can't think of a better place to spend eternity and I hope you'll visit.

All my Love

Gramps

P.S. A friend recently told me that there is a good fishing hole for trout halfway between the campsite signs of the Ice Cave and Sandy Point. Jig about a foot off bottom of the lake with a silver mooselook wobbler and you should do quite well-good luck my boy! JPC

Picking up the currency Jim counted out 10-$100 bills. Unbelieving what he had found, he counted the currency again. He then doubled the bills and tucked them into his left shirt pocket, beside his smokes. He read the letter again—a correspondence that had come from a man he'd never met!

CHAPTER XI

Yeah—right! How in the world can I leave for Allagash Lake; I've got critters to take care of and bills to pay? Besides I wouldn't even know how to get there. Jim thought and continued talking to himself. *The money will help—although it is nowhere near enough to meet my monthly obligations. Maybe I'll have to sell more livestock. Guess I could part with a house lot in the lower field though, although dad would hate for me to split up the farm.* Folding and securing the letter in his shirt pocket, beside the money and placing all of the other items back inside the trunk; he closed the lid. Jim then picked up the chest to carry it downstairs. Leaving the attic and walking through his second story bedroom on the way to a room he called the office, Jim heard a vehicle drive up and the sound of a car horn blaring from outside.

Now what? Jim wondered, listening to the fracas coming through his home's screen door. Setting the trunk down near the kitchen table he looked out a bay window to see a red GMC pickup parked in his driveway. He recognized the truck as belonging to Matt, a farming neighbor who lived a ways down the Oxbow Road. On occasion he and Matt had borrowed farm tools from each other and even helped with haying or pulling out a tractor that had gotten stuck in the mud. As near as Jim knew, Matt was honest as well as likeable. Matt had even been a pallbearer at the ceremonies for both of Jim's parents.

"What's up, Matt?" Jim asked as he walked outside, not really wanting to be disturbed at the moment.

"Oh, not too much. What are your plans for today?" The neighbor inquired.

"I've got to repair a broken hitch on the tractor, and begin turning the fields over from that whopper of a storm. I lost all of my crops but if I can get the ground ready in time I hope to do a second planting. Why, do you need a hand with something?"

"Not really. I noticed that your crops had been laid flat, my fields received damage too, but didn't get hit as hard as yours."

"Gee I am sorry to hear that Matt, but I've got a lot of stuff to do so if you don't mind I'll stop by later so we can catch up." With those words Jim turned to go back inside when Matt stopped him in midstride by asking, "You interested in selling the farm?"

Turning quickly to hear such a question coming at this

time, Jim stammered, "What, what do you mean?"

"Well, it's just that I know times have been tough with the storm and loss of your parents and all ... and my son has lost his job and he is a hard worker ..." Matt quickly continued talking, "I think he'd make a decent farmer. And I'd love to have my family closer, and I got a little money—so I thought if you were interested in selling, maybe we could make a deal? I know they would take good care of the place."

"Well I haven't really thought about it, but finances are a little tight right now. Let's go in and talk over coffee." During the first pot of the hot liquid, Jim showed Matt the letter from his grandfather, and said that he would like to get away for a while. During the second pot of coffee, Jim admitted he was intrigued by the idea of researching some of his family history. By the third carafe the two friends had reached an agreement.

Jim would rent the farm to Matt for one year, after which time Jim would have the option to reclaim his property or continue renting to Matt. Jim would keep the spare bedroom as a place to store his belongings and stay overnight whenever he needed.

Matt would pay Jim six months' rent in advance and

then the neighbor would deposit the first of each month's rent in Jim's account at the bank.

Jim would clean up his obligations and be out of the house in two weeks. He would still own the livestock, but Matt's family would take care of the animals and receive any income from the sale of milk and eggs.

Matt promised to keep the farm well maintained, to replant the crops, keep the grounds mowed, and fertilize the fields in the spring and fall.

The two shook hands and late the next day the proper papers were signed at the lawyers. Matt paid Jim the advanced rent they had agreed on. At the end of the two weeks Jim had his suitcase all packed. Just before locking the luggage shut he remembered the family scrapbook, and added that bundle of memoirs to his possessions thinking, *it might be nice to have some reading material with me.*

Jim gave the keys to the farm to Matt, and with a hint of sadness on leaving his home behind, Jim headed to Millinocket to find Dalton James. *Heck,* he thought, *maybe I can even look up Susan. We haven't talked forever.*

Matt waved good luck to his friend and watched the blue Mercury Comet disappear in a cloud of dust.

PART II

"THERE IS A PLACE; WHERE IN THE SPRING, THE FRESHWATER SMELTS ARE SO THICK, THE FISH CAN BE SCOOPED UP BY BARE HANDS."

CHAPTER XII

That evening Jim arrived in Millinocket after the town office had closed for the day, so he rented a room at the Baxter Inn. After he checked in, Jim dropped his luggage into the room and went outside to have a smoke. Thinking about all that had happened, he subconsciously pulled a cigarette from his right shirt pocket, placed it between his lips and struck a match to the tobacco. By the third puff he remembered the cancer that had claimed his father and grandfather. Not wanting to have the same experience he immediately stamped out the smoke in a nearby ashtray. Turning, he pulled out the remaining half package of cigarettes from his shirt pocket and crumpled them into the wastebasket and walked inside.

Back in the room, Jim left the TV off, and dug out his grandfather's scrapbook. He turned to the newspaper article found on the second page in the album.

FOREST FRENZY

A NEWSLETTER FROM THE ALLAGASH WOODS
A SPECIAL REPORT FOR
"THE NORTH WOODS GAZETTE"

By Tom Holt

Vol. 10, June 1975

THE YEAR THE TELOS DAM TENDER SHOT A PARROT

Jim Drake, the tender of Telos Dam, owned and operated by Bangor Hydro Company, had spent his whole life in the Maine woods. His experience goes all the way back to when he was just a lad working at sporting camps. Jim's career also included being a registered Maine guide, game warden, Allagash ranger, and several years with the U.S. Geological Survey, surveying and mapping Maine's dark forest.

The country was so ripe for discovery during that time, that the survey team even christened some of the no-name ponds that they stumbled upon. For example, one day Jim and a companion were surveying in T6R11 — north of Coffeelos Pond when they happened on a small pond. Jim's colleague asked what the body of water was called. Realizing it was an unnamed pond;

Jim replied in good humor, "It's called Imlos." And the little pool has been so-called ever since.

Some of those bodies of water are now "dying ponds" because the Black Spruce are slowly filling the wetlands and, thus, the pools have become much smaller.

Jim is known far and wide for his knowledge of the flora and fauna of the area, and was the first ranger assigned to patrol Allagash Lake. So, many years ago I called the local office of the Bangor Hydro company to arrange a visit to do an interview with their caretaker.

Leaving early in the morning I drove from my office in Bangor to learn firsthand about his early days of traipsing around the woods. Now you need to understand that his story takes place about the same time that industry was spraying the pesticide DDT, a pesticide that was so harmful to our wildlife such as bald eagles, it was eventually banned. During the DDT days, it was a rarity to see raptors and some people went for years before seeing such things as falcons.

After hours of banging over dirt roads and one flat tire, I arrived at the gate to Telos Dam. Jim was expecting me, so he had left the entry to the impoundment open and I continued driving to his camp.

When I arrived the man was standing on the lawn holding a shotgun in one hand and a dead bird in the other. The birdie was 7–8-inches long. Its wings were blue-gray with black spots and white undersides. It had a reddish-orange back with black markings. The creature's head was a bluish-gray top. And it was quite dead.

"What you got there?" I inquired.

Jim had an astonished look on his face and replied, "I think I've shot me a freaking parrot.

The woodsman explained. "I enjoy feeding and watching the wild songbirds that live in this neck of the woods. Well this morning I was watching my feathered friends at the feeding station, and it was a good start to my day because there were all kinds of birds. I saw chickadees, Gray Jays, Black-backed woodpeckers, Crossbills, and there was even a Flycatcher at the feeder.

"While I am watching, suddenly this thing here," and the man holds up the dead bird for me to see, hesitates for a moment and then continues, "swoops down and kills one of my little chickadees. Well that upset me so bad I shot the intruder with my 20 gauge. I've never seen anything like it—I think I've shot someone's parrot."

Taking a closer look I realize that he had killed a Sparrow hawk or an American kestrel. I explained that this was the smallest of the falcon species and showed him its picture from my bird book.

Jim was immediately embarrassed to make such a bad mistake and with a slight grin said, "Guess I'd better get rid of it before a warden or ranger shows up. But I won't be making such an error again. Let's go have a coffee."

Such is everyday life in the Maine woods.

JIM DRAKE, WOODSMAN, GUIDE, WARDEN, RANGER, AND DAM TENDER AT TELOS DAM FOR TEN YEARS. MARK HASKELL PHOTO. (T. CAVERLY COLLECTION.)

That night Jim Clark had another dream.

He is standing on a gravel driveway not far from the shore of a lake. Jim is dressed in a gray shirt, green pants, and wearing a forest green trail cap with a logo just over the brim—he can't quite make out the insignia. Jim is wearing his grandfather's L.L. Bean boots.

In the dream Jim is watching an equipment operator use an excavator to dig a hole. A very big hole!

CHAPTER XIII

Waking at the crack of dawn to milk the cows, Jim doesn't recognize the room or the bed he is in. Giving his mind a moment to clear away the cobwebs; Jim remembers that he's in Millinocket and why he is there.

It's too early for the town office to be open so Jim made coffee from the room's beverage maker. He pours the bitter drink into a paper hot cup and walked out to the car to follow the state road to the entrance of Baxter State Park. Passing by the dam between Ambajejus and Millinocket Lakes, he crossed the park boundary, driving by the Girl Scout camp at Natarswi. The day is so perfect he is riding with the car windows rolled down. The morning is clear and clean and the surface of lower Togue Pond is mirror smooth. Shutting the car off in the parking lot of the park's information center, Jim carries his coffee to sit at a picnic table near the beach of upper Togue. The glassy surface of the water has perfectly captured the image of the mountain and Jim wonders at the beauty of Mt. Katahdin or of Ktaadn, as Henry David Thoreau had spelled it. Somewhere out in the lake the call of a loon welcomes the day.

Driving by the scout base on his way back to town,

Jim noticed activity at the now awake girls' camp. Watching the young ladies scurry about, he remembers the good times that Susan had told him about and how much she had enjoyed the scout base as a child. With his mind now free of worry about the farm, he thinks of his friend and makes a mental promise *to call her today*.

Arriving back in Millinocket, he gets to the town office just as the clerk is unlocking the door. She greets him with a warm smile, a good morning and walks into the office to do the day's business. Once inside she opens the customer window, looks straight at Jim and asks, "May I help you?"

"I am not sure. But I am looking for someone and don't know how to find him. I was hoping you could help."

"I'll try. Who is it you're looking for?"

"Ever hear of a Dalton or Dalt James?"

The clerk opened her census book and began to follow the names in alphabetical order with her index finger. "James, James, James. I see a Dennis, a Fredrick, a Richard, a Scott, but no. ... " Then she stopped in mid-speech and with open mouth stated, "Oh, you mean DJ."

"DJ?" Jim questioned.

"Well, DJ is his nickname. Dalt's real surname is Christopher Dalton James; His first name comes from a great, great-grandfather who used to live in Sanbornton, New Hampshire. But when DJ was in elementary school he got tired of writing such a long forename so he used his middle name as a first name, and has gone by Dalton ever since. Around these parts we all just call him DJ."

"Of course I know where you can find him. Everyone in town knows DJ. He's come to the aid of more people than you can shake a stick at. I'll give you his phone number and you can call to see if he's home. I am not sure if he will be or not, cause when conditions allow he generally heads to his camp in the woods. I know he doesn't have a phone up there."

Jim borrowed the clerk's phone and dialed the 207-723 exchange. The line picked up and a message from an answering machine instructed, "If you are listening to this message that means I am not home so don't bother coming over. I'm up to my cabin near the Aroostook River. I generally come to Ashland on Tuesdays to get mail, groceries, and my newspapers. If you need to see me bad enough, on the third day of the week I always go for lunch to the Sportsman's Club

Restaurant by the Presque Isle Road between 11 A.M. and 1 P.M. I'll be wearing a green felt hat and red checkered shirt. Or if you can wait; I'll be back to my house in Millinocket after deer season." And then Jim heard the loud click of a receiver being placed on a cradle which indicated that DJ was done talking.

With farm work requiring 14-hour days, 7 days a week, Jim hadn't bothered with the calendar much. Suddenly individual days were very important. He looked at his watch and saw it was Tuesday and it was already 8:15 in the morning. Doing a quick calculation Jim figured that if he hurried he could be in Ashland by 11.

After topping off the Comet with gas, Jim headed down Route 157 intent on heading north on I95. He planned to drive to Smyrna Mill where he would take Route 212 west to Knowles Corner and turn north onto Route 11. From there he would only be about 30 miles from his destination.

Driving up the interstate Jim concentrated on what he was going to say to this man he had been told to find. The travel on the expressway was fine, but Jim got held up on Route 212. In front of him he saw that a pickup had hit a moose head-on and that the state police had stopped all traffic until the ambulance could come and retrieve the injured driver.

After what seemed forever, Jim saw the red lights of the emergency vehicle in his rearview mirror. Within 30 minutes the victim had been triaged, placed in the rescue van, and was on the way to the nearest hospital.

The police waved Jim forward and around the wrecked vehicle that had a dead bull-moose spread eagle on its hood. The animal's front hooves rested on the truck's steering wheel.

On his way once again to Ashland, Jim checked his watch and saw it was 11 A.M. on the nose. He pushed the small car to the limits, and hoped he didn't see a moose on the way.

By 11:45 A.M. Jim drove into the restaurant's parking lot, jumped out of the car and ran inside. The eatery was very busy with noontime diners, but Jim didn't see any sign of a person wearing red or having a green hat. He ordered coffee and sat down to wait.

By 1:15 P.M. DJ still hadn't showed, so Jim contemplated his next move. Thinking about driving back to Millinocket he walked to his car, and started to slide onto the seat behind the steering wheel when a buck skin brown colored GMC 4x4 pulled up and parked beside him. Watching, Jim saw an elderly man of medium height get out of the truck, wearing a red checkered shirt with a green felt fisherman's hat. Walking towards the restaurant, the gent was muttering under his breath. Jim thought he heard the man say, "Damn flat tires—I hope the joint hasn't run out of their Tuesday special."

Jim followed the man inside and watched him take a seat at the counter, as if he was used to dining alone. Jim took the stool to the man's left and asked, "Are you Dalton James?"

"Whose asking?" the man replied in a deep, clear voice that was used to speaking above the roar of wind over water.

"I think you may have known my grandfather, Jim Clark."

"Maybe I did and maybe I didn't. How's old Jim doing?" The man in the checkered shirt asked.

Surprised at the question coming from someone who was supposed to have been such a good friend to his granddad, Jim replied "why he passed away in June of 1993."

"Guess I might have known that since I was at the funeral," DJ replied sarcastically.

"Then why did you …" Jim started to inquire and then he remembered the instructions in the letter. He turned to make direct eye contact with the stranger and with a very bad French accent softly uttered, "Le moment est venu."

CHAPTER XIV

"How's that?" queried the deeply tanned woodsman. Reacting to Jim's comment, the man stiffened, stopped in mid-bite of hot turkey sandwich, and stared straight ahead at the note-covered wall behind the counter.

"Le moment est venu," repeated Jim louder.

Laying the food-filled utensil on the side of his luncheon plate, Dalton James picked up his mug and motioned for the waitress to bring more coffee, and said, "by the way, bring a cup for my friend, too." Once the cups were full of hot liquid, the old woodsman turned to face Jim.

Smiling warmly, he said, "So you've finally arrived. You're the one; your old Jim's grandson!" Then with a huge left hand he slapped Jim on the left shoulder and reached out with a firm grasp to shake the young man's right hand.

"By gosh, it's good to meet you. I was beginning to think you'd never get here. Heck, I wasn't even sure that I'd ever see you. Grab your cup and let's go over to a table, where we can talk. You oughta get something to eat to. The Tuesday blue plate specials are always good." Then he finished with a big grin, "and the waitress walks away real nice after delivering a meal." Without asking, DJ raised his hand and ordered, "Joan, he'll have a plate of the same as me, and put it on my tab."

Watching Dalt lug his plate and coffee over to a table in the back part of the restaurant, Jim followed behind. Walking closely behind the woodsman, Jim thought he could detect a slight whiff of campfire smoke. At the dining table, DJ pulled out two chairs, one for himself and one for his visitor. Sitting down he talked smoothly and quickly like he had been waiting to have this conversation.

"You know your granddad was a heck of a man, and a good friend. Yes-sir-re, one of the finest woodsmen I've ever met. He just seemed to have a natural ability; not only to find his way around the woods, but to be at the right spot at the right time. He always carried a compass, but I never saw him use it much." Here DJ paused to take a bite of lunch, which provided Jim with an opportunity to get a word in edgeways.

"I never knew him, heard lots of good stories. But I got this letter ..." and here Jim's comments were interrupted by the waitress bringing a plate of a hot food.

"Oh, I know all about the letter, I helped him write part of it."

"You helped him write it!" repeated the visitor.

- 92 -

Temporarily silenced by the revelation, Jim quickly realized that he had found the right man. Then suddenly, a torrent of questions flowed from the young caller, rolling off his tongue like a flooded brook after a heavy rain.

"What was he like? Did you meet him on Allagash Lake? Did you used to travel with him into the woods? What did you mean that he was always at the right place at the right time? The letter said that I had to go to Allagash Lake, do you know why?"

Jim spoke so fast and DJ listened intently, as if he had been anticipating these questions for a very long time. When Jim stopped talking long enough to take a breath, the woodsman offered, "What do you say we have a piece of apple pie and vanilla bean ice cream? It is very good here. After eating we'll drive out to my camp on the Aroostook River. We can talk on the way. You got a sleeping bag?" Without waiting for an answer DJ continued.

"Never mind, I've got extra. Don't need to bring food either, I've got plenty. You ever eaten fresh brook trout and canned fiddleheads? Got some canned moose meat, too." Standing, the woodsman paid their bill and walked towards his truck, confident that Jim would follow.

Jim nodded ok and asked, "What do I do with my car?"

"You can leave it right off to the side of the parking lot, over there next to the lawn. Nobody will bother it. Just leave the keys with Joan in case they need to move it."

Jim moved the blue vehicle as instructed and walked inside to drop off the keys. Handing them over to the waitress he remembered his promise and inquired, "Is there a pay telephone handy? I'd like to make a call."

Joan responded, "Figured you wanted to talk to someone, or you wouldn't have asked for the phone. It's over there by the lavatory."

Walking by the door to the men's room, Jim picked up the receiver and dialed a phone number that he'd kept tucked in his wallet.

An answering machine picked up the call and a voice on the other end said, "Hi, This is Susan and you've reached the home of the King family. My parents aren't in right now, so if you want to talk to them; you'll have to call back. If you want to speak with me, I am away this summer working as a counselor at Camp Natarswi. You're welcome to visit, but I may be out in the woods guiding scouts. I'll be home in the fall though to teach school." Then a cheery voice on the line ended with, "Thanks for calling."

Jim couldn't help but worry as he wondered how she might react to hearing from him after such a long time. But he left the following message anyway.

"Hi Susan, This is Jim. I, aaah, well, I wanted, ahhh, I mean, I am sorry I haven't had time to call but I've been really busy and now I have to go into the Allagash country for a few days. I'll try calling when I get back out of the woods." Then Jim said, "I've had so much going on, and I feel bad that I haven't talked with you before now. I hope you are well." Then in a soft voice almost too low for anyone to hear he finished his message with, "I, I miss you, 'bye."

Figures, thought Jim. Grabbing his suitcase out of the car he walked towards the idling four-wheel drive, and reasoned *I must have driven right past her this morning— wonder if she's married?*

Jumping into the passenger's seat of Dalton's truck, Jim began buckling his seat belt when he felt something cold and wet in his left ear. Turning quickly he saw intelligent eyes looking back at him over a long nose and a panting pink tongue.

DJ made the introductions: "Jim meet Misty, Misty meet Jim. He's going to be staying with us for a few days."

Greeting the newcomer in her own way, the dog put her nose under Jim's hand and lifted it up as if to suggest "seeing how you aren't doing anything right now, you might just as well pat me."

While Jim scratched the dog's ear Dalton talked about his pet golden retriever. "Misty's pedigree name is Katahdin's Allagash Mist; I call her Misty for short. She's my best friend, a great hunter, and always lets me know whenever there is a bear around."

CHAPTER XV

Heading west out of the restaurant's parking lot, Dalton turned into the driveway of the closest convenience store and pulled up to the only gas pump in town. Explaining, the old man said, "I always top off my tank before heading into the woods. Got some gas at camp, but like to keep it for an emergency. If there is anything you need, now is the time to get it. We won't be back out to town for a week."

Not knowing what was ahead Jim thought about buying one last pack of cigarettes but changed his mind with, *No–guess I won't. I stopped smoking once and this is as good as time as any to stay quit.*

Driving south on Route 11 Jim asked where they were headed. Dalton replied by pulling an atlas out of the pouch on the back of Jim's seat, handed it to the passenger and said, "Open to page 56. When you get there look at the left side of the page until you see the letter D. Then draw an imaginary line from the letter D toward the east. Now look at the top of the page until you see the number 3. Good, now draw another imaginary line south." Watching the young man follow his instructions, DJ then said, "My camp is right where those lines intersect. It's not far as the crow flies, but then again—we ain't crows. The cabin is on Carpenter Pond and I stay there most of the year; unless I get an assignment."

Assignment? Jim wondered, but when Dalton didn't offer to elaborate the passenger decided to change the subject. "About how long will it take us by vehicle?" Jim asked.

"About three hours and that is if we don't have a flat tire, hit a moose, deer, or some other critter." Grinning, Dalton continued, "If we hit venison then it will take us a while longer cause of the time it takes to do the skinning and quartering."

Jim knew that it was off season for possessing wild game so he figured *and hoped* that his new friend was kidding. But he wasn't really sure.

Dalton continued explaining their route. "We'll drive down 11 for a ways and then head west through the Oxbow Gate run by the North Maine Woods. Going that way is a little like going around Robin Hood's Barn, but there is less traffic and we'll have a better chance of seeing animals. My place is a nice spot, and from my porch I can be to Allagash Lake within a reasonable amount of time."

Their conversation remained light, with no mention of the task that Jim had expected to hear about. Finally turning onto a grass driveway, they arrived at Carpenter Pond in time to lug the groceries and other supplies into camp before dark. Jim took note of the place where he would be apparently staying for the next seven days. Sitting in the middle of a manicured lawn, the camp was classic spruce log construction, with an open porch that faced south. The roof was shingled with cedar shakes, and a fieldstone chimney centered on the north wall ensured they would be warm during cold nights. There were enough windows on all sides to allow for the inside to remain light and cheery. Under the eve along one outside wall there were two fly rods waiting on nails driven into the rounded logs.

Stepping onto the porch Jim noticed that there was a propane refrigerator sitting within easy reach from the interior door. On the inside of the exterior wall of the overhang, a workbench held assorted tools, all organized in proper order. Entering the camp, the interior was so well arranged that the one room residence looked bigger than what a person would expect.

Along one wall rested a shiny, black, cast iron sink. Above the sink sat a large window positioned so that whoever was working at the basin could enjoy a panoramic view of the lake. The room was made cheerier because all the windows of the building were framed by bright yellow curtains. Beside the sink was a four-burner propane stove, on which on Dalton began boiling a handful of tea.

Across the room on the opposite wall sat a Star Kineo woodstove. The antique cook stove's black top, oven door, and chrome trim were polished to perfection. Jim thought, *Yup, ready to make coffee, cook an apple pie, or to heat water in the stove's copper water tank; I'd say.*

Halfway between the stove and sink sat a kitchen table, around which sat four captain's chairs, waiting for company. A couch and assorted rocking chairs were placed about the room; for comfort and for conversation.

Along the back wall were two sets of double-wide bunk beds. All of the bunks were made up with blankets and pillows in case unexpected company arrived. Setting his suitcase on one of the bottom bunks, Jim took the cup of tea that DJ offered and walked outside to the entryway. Easing into a rocking chair on the porch, Jim thought that the lake at the end of a well-worn path *is one of the prettiest I've ever seen.*

While Jim enjoyed the night air, the loons on the lake offered their prediction for the coming weather. Inside the cabin he could hear Dalton moving furniture. A closet door opened and closed; then Jim heard the man's footsteps coming closer.

Coming through the interior door, DJ handed Jim a carbine.

Setting his tea aside and accepting the gun, Jim asked, "What's this?"

"A rifle," the woodsman replied.

"Guess I could tell that, why are you handing it to me?"

"It's a Marlin 38–40."

"Are you giving it to me?"

"Can't, it's not mine."

"Whose is it?" Jim asked.

"Yours," DJ stated enjoying the little game he was playing with the new kid.

"Guess I don't know what you mean."

Deciding to explain, Dalton replied, "This gun is a Model 94, 38–40 carbine that shoots an 180 grain bullet at 1,160 feet per second. The gun was patented in 1893 and has been in one family for over 100 years. It was once used to shoot nuisance deer out of an apple orchard on a farm outside of Skowhegan. Then a long time ago, a woman in Cornville used it to finish off a porcupine that was trying to get to the family's dog kennel."

MODEL 94, 38–40 CARBINE. PATENTED 1893. T.CAVERLY PHOTO.

Remembering the shells in his grandfather's trunk, Jim knew this must be the family gun; the one he had always heard about. "But how did you …,

"Why is it …, Is this why I am here? Is this the heirloom I am supposed to retrieve?" Questions were coming to Jim's mind faster than his tongue would work.

"Well son, I've been keeping it for you. It's yours now. But it's been a long day; let's call it a night and I'll explain tomorrow." Without waiting for approval, and taking one last look towards the evening sky, the tired man shuffled through the inside door and off to a bunk by the nearest window. Misty followed behind and took her place on a rug at the foot of the bed.

Jim held the rifle for what seemed like hours. The stock of the gun was a warm brown and by touching it, Jim thought he could feel the history of the Clark family flowing through his veins. Not feeling tired and spying a nearby newspaper on the table, Jim picked it up and read:

FOREST FRENZY

A NEWSLETTER FROM THE ALLAGASH WOODS

SPECIAL REPORT FOR

"THE NORTH WOODS GAZETTE"

By Tom Holt

Vol. 12, June 1977

THE DAY THE RANGER FELL OUT OF THE CANOE

As a special-to-the-paper reporter covering the Allagash, I meet tons of nice people and very dedicated rangers; often becoming close friends after just a few days together. Such was the case with a recent visit with the assistant ranger at Round Pond in T13R12.

By calling the radio dispatch for the Allagash Wilderness Waterway, I was able to make arrangements to travel to Round Pond to spend a few days with this young man and accompany him on his routine patrol. There isn't a road access to the pond so I had to make arrangements to be picked up by canoe. So I spoke to the dispatcher on the phone and she relayed my request to the man on the ground that had a radio call sign of 1713.

The conversation went over the air as follows:

"Ashland to 1713"

"1713–10-3." (I later learned that 10-3 meant that it was ok for the operator to proceed.)

"I have a Mr. Holt on the phone. He is a reporter from the newspaper who would like to come in for a visit."

"That's fine, Ashland. I have been expecting his call. And he is welcome to meet me at Henderson Brook Bridge. Does he have an ETA? And will he being staying overnight?"

"Mr. Holt said he can be at the bridge at 1 P.M. tomorrow, and yes, he would like to stay for two nights."

"10-4 (which means ok), I'll meet him at the bridge tomorrow at 1 P.M. Tell him to bring a raincoat and life preserver."

"10-4, Ashland clear."

The following day I was at the bridge when I heard a canoe and motor coming up the river where we had made arrangements to meet. The hum of the motor was coming up river strong when the sound seemed to turn and begin to fade away. As I listened the whine of the motor seemed to once again grow strong, only to weaken. This happened several times before I finally could see the ranger motoring my way in his 20-foot Grumman canoe with a 10-hp Mercury outboard hanging off the side.

When he got close to the landing, in one smooth

swoop he shut off the outboard, raised it so the foot of the motor was off the ground. He then grabbed a 12-foot canoe pole and eased the bow onto shore so easily that the metal barely made a sound on the gravel. I could see that he was soaking wet.

Waving me a hello with his right hand, He asked "did you hear my motor?"

"Yes," I responded. "I couldn't tell if you were coming or going."

"Well, I kinda was doing both."

"How so," I asked.

Below is the ranger's story as told to me.

"The channel in this section of river can be hard to see so on my way to meet you I was standing up in the canoe so I could better see any obstacles in the water. About 20 minutes from the bridge I spied something white, partially submerged in the water, on the far side of the river.

"I was staring at it trying to figure out if the object was someone's lost gear or some white foam. While trying to determine if I should go over, the outboard's propeller hit a sunken log on the bottom of the river. That collision with the log caused the bow of my canoe to swing downstream so quickly that I lost my grip on the handle of the outboard and I was thrown out of the canoe.

"The water where I landed was about waist deep and I stood there and watched my Grumman drive away. But the motor is still turned so the canoe makes a big circle and comes right back by me. I missed the first pass, but on its second go-around I was able to grab the

side of my canoe and jump in."
I then loaded my gear in the canoe with my new ranger friend and spent two marvelous days on the river.

Such is everyday life in the Maine woods.

Finally feeling sleepy, Jim quietly headed off to his own bed, laid the rifle on the bunk between him and the wall for safety, and fell asleep to the soft snores of Dalton James and Misty coming from across the room.

That night Jim had another dream.

CHAPTER XVI

He is standing on a driveway not far from the shore of a lake; he can see the swirls of trout feeding on the Mayflies flying over the surface of the water. Jim is dressed in a gray shirt, green pants, and wearing a forest green trail cap with a logo just over the brim—he can't quite make out the insignia. Jim is wearing his grandfather's L.L. Bean boots.

In the vision Jim is watching a construction crew pour concrete into forms placed around a big hole in the ground. Another man, standing nearby, is wearing the same clothes as Jim. The stranger is holding a set of blueprints and talking intently.

A hot breath in Jim's face brings him out of the dream. Misty is standing there wagging her tail in the pet's special way of an early morning greeting. Jim reaches out to pat the dog when Dalton hollers, "Come on, Misty—we've got to go get some firewood. Coffee is ready Jim."

Dressed, Jim walks over to the gas range to pour the hot morning liquid into a waiting mug. Jim turns when he hears the dog's claws tapping across the wooden planks of the porch floor. Misty walks back into the room with her head held high carrying a small stick of hardwood in her mouth. The pet crosses to the wood box and drops the fuel inside. Dalt, carrying an armful of biscuit wood, follows the dog and adds that to the day's supply of firewood. Jim takes a seat at the table just as Dalt places plates of eggs, bacon, beans, and home fries on the oak table. After the two men eat, Misty polishes off any empty dishes that are offered.

The next seven days went quicker than Jim could ever imagine. During the day Dalt would teach Jim about life in the outdoors. This included how to take care of propane appliances; the proper way to operate and maintain a canoe and motor; the right way to read maps and to use a compass; the 10 and 2 o'clock positions to use when holding a fly rod; and how to choose the right fly to use to attract "even the fussiest trout"; and the best way to build an outside warming fire—even in the pouring rain.

After testing Jim about his knowledge of the basics of canoe operation, Dalton refined the tutorials. Dalt demonstrated how to use a chain saw to make a motor-mount from a junk of yellow birch log. Once the support was fastened to the left side of the 20-foot canoe, then there was the proper way to hang the 80-lb. outboard. "It was important," Dalt had said, "that the motor is low enough in the water for the cooling water pump to pick up water, but not so deep that the keel of the outboard grounds out on a river's gravel bars."

Once the motor was on the canoe, there was the lecture about the balancing of the motor, gas tank, and gear—so the whole load would travel steady across a lake or up a river.

Then there was poling—sometimes there wasn't enough water to use the outboard or to paddle, so poling was required. As DJ explained, "The ability of using a 12-foot spruce snubbing staff to propel a canoe upstream, or to snub your craft downstream is an art all by itself." Dalton then described the proper loading of a canoe for poling in a river. "A canoe acts like a weathervane in the wind," DJ continued, "its heavy end will turn with the current. So when poling upstream the stern should be loaded heavy, and thus, when snubbing downstream the bow should be heavier."

At night, Jim was asking one question after another; Dalt provided answers and answered them as fast as they were asked.

Jim was told about the friendship between this new friend and his grandfather—so close they felt like brothers. That they had first met one spring when Dalton's canoe had capsized on Allagash Lake. At the time Dalton had been a newly appointed ranger for the Department of Conservation and was on routine patrol when a crosswind caught him by surprise. Dalton hadn't been wearing his lifejacket and the water was cold; very, very cold. Jim's granddad had been coming onto the lake from upper Allagash Stream and arrived at the inlet just as Dalt went over.

By the time that Jim's grandfather got to Dalt; the young ranger was near hypothermic. Jim's grandfather had pulled the wet man into his canoe, paddled him to the ranger's camp, and wrapped the shivering man in warm blankets. He then made coffee for Dalt and instructed, "get out of those clothes and I'll be back shortly."

Then Jim's grandfather paddled back to the swamped canoe, bailed out enough water so the craft would float and towed it back and tied the patrol canoe off at the ranger's dock. While Dalton was recovering inside the camp, the grandfather had dried out the canoe and got the outboard motor back into running condition.

Dalt explained how that started a friendship that lasted for years. The two spoke often by phone, suggesting and planning trips. Even during the winter when Dalton was home for the season, they would talk weekly and make plans for the coming summer.

Then one year Jim's grandfather had come in and camped by the Ice Caves, his final visit to the lake. That summer there had been a lot of bear trouble around the lake, and DJ had asked the grandfather to bring in a rifle so they could dispatch the bear. The grandfather brought in a family heirloom a Marlin 38–40 carbine. A terrible thunderstorm came through and Dalton insisted that the grandfather come over to the camp to wait out the storm. The tempest lasted for several days.

"After the wind blew out we returned back to the campsite to see how your grandfather's tent had held up. On the way we crossed the trail to the Ice Caves and heard a strange sound coming out of the holes of the geological formation. And those sounds, how they are created are the reasons you must to go to Allagash Lake.

"Do you remember in the letter when your granddad said he didn't wanna ask your parents to retrieve his belongings? Well there is a little more to the story. That is why you need to go to the Ice Caves and there is where you'll find the heirloom you seek."

CHAPTER XVII

Jim's visit had been the quickest seven days he'd ever seen. At dawn of the next day Jim woke to the sound of pots and pans rattling near the kitchen stove. Throwing off the bedcovers, he looked over to see DJ at the stove rattling up a breakfast of beans, biscuits, and bacon. Without looking up from his cooking DJ asked, "You interested in going for a ride?"

"Where to? Thought I had to leave today—with being here a week and all?"

"I kinda thought we might head over Allagash Lake way today. Actually I am supposed to report for work by tomorrow."

"Oh! What kind of work?" Jim inquired.

"The Waterway supervisor is a friend of mine and a short time before you arrived last week, he had sent me a letter. It appears that the current ranger was called home to deal with a family emergency. In the correspondence, the supervisor said he had coverage on the lake for a short time, but needed a fill-in uniform for several days. I used to work for him as a ranger on the waterway several years ago and he knows me, my work, and appreciates that I understand the moods of the lake.

"He'd written to ask if I'd be willing to stay there for a couple of weeks. I've called him and told him I could. I am supposed to begin patrolling the lake by tomorrow morning."

Without waiting for Jim's answer the once-retired ranger continued, "if you can stay a while, we'll go into town, pick up a few supplies, and find you a proper pack, sleeping bag, compass, waterproof match case, belt knife, a bottle of the sportsman's friend, "Ole Time Woodsman's Fly Dope," and a new cruising ax.

"Well I suppose I could," Jim said hesitating and then realizing, *the farm is all set for a while, so guess I've really got nothing to hurry back for.* And then he remembered Susan.

"Sure I can go, but I need to make a couple of phone calls first. Wouldn't mind getting a haircut either."

Once in town, while DJ was shopping, Jim first called Matt to let him know he would be out of touch by phone for several days and Matt assured Jim that everything was fine at the farm.

Then Jim tried calling Susan again. When he heard the answering machine pick up and her voice say, "Hi, this is Susan and you've reach the home of …" he hung up. Jim wasn't sure how Susan had reacted to his last message or if she had even heard it. He didn't dare to leave another.

Turning away from the phone at the store, Jim saw Dalton filling coolers with ice and enough food to last for at least a couple of weeks. By the time the shopping was all done, DJ suggested that they stop by the restaurant for an early lunch before heading into the woods.

Walking through the door of the café, Jim noticed that the eatery was already busy. By the looks of the various sort of dress there were woods workers, game wardens, forest rangers, sport fishermen, and vacationers, all in various stages of chowing down. Sitting alone at the counter was someone wearing an outfit so shabby that the clothing appeared to have been worn for days. Yawning, the man looked like someone who had been up all night. Dalton took the stool next to this individual who was staring at his meal. "This meat is tougher than a woodpecker's beak, why I couldn't even chew this gristle with George Washington's teeth," the man griped.

With a wink at Jim, DJ turned to the person doing the complaining and said, "Good morning George, how are things this fine day?" Without replying George sniffed the air and muttered, "must be a ranger or some other such waste of our tax payers' dollar nearby—I can smell him."

Ignoring the insult, Dalton continued, "Our day has started off pretty well; even saw a couple deer on the way into town this morning. How's your week going?"

George replied, "Was going good until a couple of minutes ago. Saw deer you say, did you shoot 'em? I could use some camp meat."

"Nope, it's not hunting season, you know. One of the deer was nursing the cutest fawn, all covered with white spots the little guy was."

"Good to hear about the lamb, he'll be more veal for my freezer."

Still trying to make conversation, DJ gave it one last try, "you headed into Allagash Lake anytime soon?"

"Nope—no need to go there." And then with a sideways look at Dalton, George asked, "you gonna be in that way?"

"Yup, the supervisor has asked me to fill in for a while."

Under his breath Jim thought he heard George say, "Crap," and then in a louder voice ask—"how long 'fore you're goin' in?"

"No hurry, really. Probably head that way in three or four days."

"Well, I hope your canoe sinks." And with that George pushed his plate back, threw a $10 bill on the table, and stormed out the door.

"Friendly sort isn't he?" Jim observed.

"Not at all," Dalton replied. "That's George and he's the biggest poacher there is in the north woods. He and I had a run in a few years ago while I was rangering and he's never forgotten it. If you run across any skullduggery in that country, more than likely George will be involved—what do ya say we head to the lake? I'd like to reach camp before dark."

"I thought you told George you weren't heading in for a while?"

"I did, but just to throw him off. I hate telling him a white lie, but it doesn't pay to let George know when, where, or what I'll be doing at any given time."

FOREST FRENZY

A NEWSLETTER FROM THE ALLAGASH WOODS

SPECIAL REPORT FOR

"THE NORTH WOODS GAZETTE"

by Tom Holt

Vol. 13, June 1978

WILDLIFE CONVERSATION

My selection for this piece comes directly from the crown of the wilderness river corridor from whence the river gets its name, "Allagaskwigamook or Allagash Lake." For this report I decided to go on my own into the Maine woods. In my previous visits I had spent time listening and learning from the people who work there — from the ones who call the woods home; and I had learned — oh, how I had learned!

So my plan was to drive to the put-in at upper Allagash Stream, canoe down the stream and if the site was open, camp for the night at the Ledges tent site on the north end of the lake. I was quite proud when my efforts were successful and I arrived without incident to the "Ledges." In a short time I had my nylon shelter up and cooking a delicious (new to me) receipt I'd discovered known as a tinfoil dinner.

After eating I took a short paddle around my section of the lake. I was pleased to find there was an ample supply of wildlife. Brook trout were rising in abundance, the terns and Bonaparte gulls were having a conversation near a place called Tern Island. Overhead an immature bald eagle surveyed its domain by soaring on the thermal updrafts lifting off the lake. On shore a whitetail splashed in the shallows as it fed on the tender buds of the wild rose bush.

Feeling tired from so much fresh air I decided to call it a night. About 10 o'clock I heeded the call of nature. When I stepped outside of the tent, I was surprised to find the brightness of the evening constellations. Directly overhead the Big Dipper, with the North Star in the handle, shone so vivid and seemed so close, that it seemed that if I stood on the picnic table and reached really high — I could touch the sky.

Absorbing the evening sky for quite a while, it was time to return to the comfort of my sleeping bag. But before I fell asleep a local Barred owl decided it was time for an evening hunt. The bird of prey began issuing it's call of "Who cooks for you? Who, who cooks for you at all?"

Soon the Barred owl was answered by the deep hooting voice of the Great Horned owl issuing his "hoo-h'Hoo–hoo." And so it became a two-way conversation as in the following: "Who cooks for you? Who, who cooks for you at all?" "Hoo–h'Hoo?"

And then the conversation repeated, "Who cooks for you? "Who, who cooks for you at all?" Again followed by, "Hoo–h'Hoo?"

This exchange went on for some time, reminding me of nature's equivalent of the famous Abbott and Costello routine of, "Who's on first?"

That night I had the best night sleep in years and I felt like I was in a place where I'd discovered an inner peace.

Such is everyday life in the Maine woods.

PART III

"There is a place; where the pink, white, and yellow lady slippers grow so thick—the orchids blanket the ground like a decorative quilt."

CHAPTER XVIII

After they arrived back at camp, Jim helped load Dalton's 20-foot Atkinson Traveler onto the vehicle's canoe racks, then, while DJ packed enough supplies and equipment to last several days; Jim arranged his personal effects into a brand new waterproof canoe bag—in preparation for a trip across water.

Back on the road they drove towards the deep woods, "In fact, we are going so far into the forest," Dalton had joked, "that once we get there, no matter which direction we travel, we're headed back to town." Hearing the yarn before, Misty ignored her master's comment and stared out the backseat window to watch for partridge.

Dalt continued to explain their journey ahead. "The place where we're headed, is a spot that old Jim held in high esteem. Allegash Lake, as naturalist Henry David Thoreau called the place, is the crown jewel of the Waterway. The Lake is special because it is the one place in the corridor where folks can experience the best of our natural world; free of motors of any kind. Combustible engines aren't allowed on the water or within one mile of the remote corridor from May to October. So anytime a person is there, they are experiencing the finest outdoor experience that Mother Nature has to offer.

"Once we've reached the put-in at upper Allagash Stream, the three of us will travel downstream to an old game warden camp, where we'll be staying. The residence isn't far from the inlet, and within sight of the busiest entrance to the lake." Listening intently, Jim remained quiet so as not to provide any interruption to his host.

So the guide continued, "For years the Waterway has borrowed the facility so the ranger could be 'near the action.' Whether it's parties that arrived for fishing, paddling, or on a pilgrimage to Allagash Village, the camp is as good a spot as any to keep an eye on whoever is coming or going."

Finally arriving at the landing, Dalt grunted when he saw an old truck already there.

"Do you know whose it is?" Jim asked as he pointed towards the jalopy.

"Certainly do." Replied Dalt and Jim noticed that his friend's jaw tighten when he realized who was nearby. "I've seen the old crate way too often to suit my tastes. It's George's."

"Why is he here?"

"Because he thinks I won't be. Let's head to the lake to see what we find."

Taking a closer look at the automobile, Jim thought the faded green pickup appeared to be something that had been driven too fast, for too many years, over too many rough and muddy roads. The rust holes in the fenders had been covered by colored patches of duct tape. The rear bumper hung low and loose on the driver's side, and on the passenger's side the right rear fender had broken free of its braces. Below the fender a shock absorber hung lifeless. And there were other repairs that should have been made. The front windshield showed spider-web-like cracks throughout. The glass of the right passenger's side window was missing and the opening, where the pane should have been, had been covered by a piece of heavy-duty, milky white plastic—held in place by the same adhesive tape as on the fenders. The headlight on the driver's side was broken and a worn-out brake light hung with its wires exposed on the opposite back corner.

An unpainted canoe rack on the bed of the truck completed the portrait of a piece of equipment that wasn't maintained very well.

Then, almost by accident Jim noticed something else. The junky-looking vehicle had new tires and not cheap ones either, but solid rubber that would get a man in and out of the woods. And then there was the inside of the truck. Peeking through dirty windows, Jim expected to see empty beer and soda bottles and other trash discarded onto the floorboards and an interior that was torn and dirty. But what he found was an inside of a vehicle that was exceptionally clean and well organized; the exact opposite of the picture the exterior portrayed. Wondering silently about the two extremes in appearance of the truck, Jim walked over to help DJ unload.

After removing the canoe from the racks, the two men followed a grassy trail to the water's edge, where the "Traveler" floated gently, and very much at home. While stowing their gear "just so" in the canoe, Dalton explained why they needed to take his canoe. "There is a 20-foot aluminum canoe with an outboard waiting at camp for to us work from, but I wanna take mine just in case we feel like doing some evening fishing. Nothing better than casting on a lake when the water is flat calm and the squaretails are feeding." Continuing, DJ explained why he thought the canoe was unique. "Modeled after the famous E.M. White craft, the canoe is made right here in Maine by the Northwood's Canoe Company. Once we place the craft in the water you'll find that my pride and joy resembles a floating sculpture that maneuvers quickly in rapids and tracks straight and true on a lake or pond.

"It will take us about an hour to get to where the stream enters the lake, and while you have a paddle, it won't be needed until we get to Johnson Stream. Just relax and let me do the work until we get there. I'll let you know when to start paddling."

With Jim seated in the bow, and the golden retriever in her assigned place between Dalton's feet in the stern; the guide picked up his canoe pole and began working their way down stream.

Not required to do any work, Jim observed his surroundings. The first thing the young man noticed was the feel of the corridor. The air was clean, and carried the resinous fragrance of white cedar. Even during the heat of the day, the water in the bubbling stream was clear and cool. Floating by the banks of the boreal forest, the bowman watched the leaf of the matured ostrich fern wave a gentle hello at their passing. Jim felt as though he was experiencing the Maine woods just as the old time trappers and voyagers must have done eons ago—at the dawn of time. Now, this is the proper way to begin a canoe trip, he thought.

Jim could hear the clink of the steel shoe on the end of

Dalt's snubbing pole as the tool picked out just the right spot on the streambed from which to guide the canoe. Missing rock after rock, the canoeist expertly found the deepest channel; and thus protected his canoe from running onto any hidden obstacles.

As Jim beheld his surroundings there was a sudden crash and he turned in time to see the white flash from the tail of a startled buck as the whitetail deer bound over a low bush and immediately disappeared out of sight of the intruders.

Floating along, the local wildlife continued to allow their presence to be observed. Jim saw a sleepy wood turtle dozing in the afternoon sun on top of a partly submerged log. In biology class Jim had learned these small stream dwellers had dark gray to solid black heads with a neck, chin, and legs of orange to red in color, with faint yellow stripes. The turtle could be recognized by the pyramidal pattern of ridges and grooves on its shell. He had also read that the amphibians loved clear streams with firm, sandy bottoms. A natural monitor of the cleanliness of the environment, similar to a canary in a coal mine; the reptile preferred clean air and water and didn't adjust very well to the destruction of its ecological habitat.

Around the first corner, a young calf moose stared at

the travelers, as if it could smell the strangers but couldn't see them very well. Behind a submerged rock, a speckled-colored brook trout waved its square tail back and forth, watching and waiting for an afternoon snack of the caddis fly nymph to float by.

Finally arriving in front of a small muddy bottom brook on river right, Dalton pointed at the flowage and explained, "This is the confluence where Johnson Stream meets Allagash Stream. From here on out the watercourse is deep enough to paddle, so go ahead and help out."

Continuing, the guide pointed up the mud rivulet and offered, "It's about a mile up that little tributary to Johnson Pond. The pond is one of the most popular ways for folks to get into Allagash Lake. Johnson used to be a very busy spot for flying services to drop off sports with their canoes. But several years ago, the Federal Aviation Administration, or FAA, ruled that floatplanes couldn't carry passengers with canoes strapped to the pontoons. Because of that regulation and the increased cost of gasoline, most folks now drive to Johnson Pond to begin their trip. Leaving their vehicle behind, the travelers hire a transport service to move their automobile to the village."

"Don't look like much of a stream," Jim observed, looking at the brook's trickle.

"Guess it doesn't. But most of the flow has a sandy streambed and there are six beaver dams between here and Johnson. When parties leave the pond; they just kick a hole in each dam they come to. That generally provides enough water to float to the next bushy impoundment. There is still some dragging, and muddy walking but the flowage provides access to the lake. I prefer the upper stream myself. Once on the lake, it is only about two hours back to my vehicle and that means that my truck is handy. Not to mention the stream is a nicer way to travel, both down and up."

With two people now paddling, the canoe glided easily downstream with the gentle current. Jim noticed that the wind in the trees was starting to pick up and so he predicted they were getting close to the lake. Then he heard a resounding splash coming from around a distant corner—sounding much like a very large beaver slapping its tail.

Easing around a bend, Jim looked to river left and saw a high, gray, stone outcropping that sloped toward the stream. The center of the ledge was completely wet and looked like a cloud burst had just dropped a ton of rain. Then Jim saw it. A black bear was climbing out of the stream, and walking up along the edge of the outcrop until the bruin reached the top. Once there, the animal first looked around to see if anyone was watching, and then sat down on the watery trail, using the stone like a north woods slide to ride his way into the water. Jim wasn't sure, but the bear looked amused and seemed to be smiling.

BEAR SLIDING ON A LEDGE

With a big grin on his face DJ said, "Well, my friend, welcome to Allagash Lake."

Jim turned to look straight ahead and saw it.

CHAPTER XIX

The newcomer stared in awe at the peaks and valleys of the inland sea that rolled and dipped before him. Against a distant horizon Jim saw blue waves that proudly sported whitecaps only to have crest after crest fracture when their watery momentum was interrupted by the multitude of rock strewn islands.

Dalt pointed at an object across the body of water toward a tree that stood tall above the rest of the forest and said, "See that bushy-topped pine on the distant eastern horizon?" Jim nodded yes, so the guide continued … "well, that evergreen marks the outlet of the lake, it's about three miles away."

"Wow, this lake is bigger than I thought it would be," said Jim.

"And you're only seeing part of it. Once you swing around that point of land to the south, the surface goes on for another four miles and meets the portage trail to Round Pond. That end of the lake is also where the watchman lives who staffs the fire tower on Allagash Mountain.

"If you look close just to the east side of the closest

island—there, just to our right, you can make out a canoe tied to a dock—that's where we'll be staying. We'll get there eventually, but for now we have a situation to deal with." With that observation, Dalt pointed to the left at a campsite near a rock outcropping.

"That is the Ledges Campsite and it looks like we have a visitor."

Following to Dalton's gaze, Jim could see an empty aluminum canoe with a black outboard motor sitting on shore near the campsite. Guess we'll head on over—I know that canoe and it doesn't belong to the state."

"How do you know? It looks identical to the one at the dock."

"I recognize the craft as one I've seen before. It is another little trick from our friend. A while back George bought a canoe to mimic the ones the state uses for patrol. That way when a ranger is away, he can motor on the lake at will and folks won't be the wiser that he is illegal."

Nearing the campsite, Jim saw Dalt square his shoulders as if getting ready for a physical confrontation. In the distance they could hear the runnnn, runnn, runnnn of a chainsaw. Using his snubbing pole, Dalt eased onto the pebble beach.

After the canoe had lightly touched down, Jim moved out of the bow and pulled the craft onto the landing. Instructing Misty to stay, Dalt stepped onto shore, and walked toward the sound. The golden retriever sat and stared at her master, ready to come if needed.

Appraising the visitor's canoe, Jim noticed that from first appearance the outer shell of the 20-foot canoe was beat up and portrayed lots of dings, dents, and scratches. It was plainly a piece of equipment that had been used hard and when it became used up and mostly junk—the aluminum boat was meant to be discarded. But looking beyond the exterior of the watery vehicle, Jim saw a different picture.

On the interior of the canoe each piece of equipment was stored in a very careful manner. The ash canoe paddle had a new coat of varnish, the 12-foot snubbing pole was straight and true. George even had stamped his name in the steel shoe that protected the bottom of the pole. The gas tank was clean without any sign of there ever being a fuel spillage. The outboard motor hung true and straight and the prop looked brand new, like the motor had never hit a gravel bar or rock in the river. And the bottom of the canoe was completely clean, and appeared like its occupant had never stepped in with muddy shoes. Quite an opposite appearance, Jim observed and then turned to keep up with Dalt.

Following the noise the two men soon found George, the person Jim had seen earlier in the restaurant; working in earnest at cutting live trees. George never saw the two coming.

Not wanting to get to surprise a man using a chain saw, Dalton picked up a small spruce cone from the compacted ground, and threw it at the back of George. The cutter didn't turn around so Dalton threw another, hitting the man on the back of the neck. This time George looked back over his shoulder—directly into a torrent of daggers flowing out of Dalton's eyes. George shut off the chain saw and set the equipment on the ground and turned as Dalton asked …

"What you doing George?"

Caught off guard the man stammered, "I thought you weren't coming in for a few days. I thought that I'd …"

"Have time to get your project done before I arrived?" Dalt said finishing his adversary's sentence.

"I expected to be out … I mean to be upstream before …"

"What are you doing here anyway," Dalton commanded

as he stopped George short and assumed the role of being in charge.

"I'm clearing a trail to the road that comes in by Mile Pond. That way I can walk my sports into the campsite without having to drag down that pesky stream. Ain't that a good idea?"

"No, that's not a good idea and you know it. This is a canoeing corridor and people need to feel secure in their campsite without worrying about someone hiking in to check 'em out. Once again, George, you are violating several regulations, most of which you've been warned about before."

For once George remained quiet so Dalton continued, "Let's see, first infraction is that you used a chainsaw in a wilderness area without permission, second, you've attempted to establish a hiking trail into a designated canoe trail, and third, there is the unauthorized cutting of live trees not to mention using an outboard motor in prohibited waters. I also saw a fishing rod with a bobber in the stern of your canoe when I walked by. So I suspect if I'd come by a little later I would have seen you fishing with worms in a lake where only artificial lures are allowed."

By now George had regained his composure, curled his upper lip, and sneered, "so what you gonna do about it Mr. reeetirrred ranger dirt bag?" And then George followed with, "and don't be thinking I'm showing you any ID 'cause I just don't have a thing that proves who I am."

"Guess you knew that because of my retirement, I had to turn in my ticket books. But you see, George that really doesn't matter because I can still file a report with the Chamberlain Lake ranger or the local game warden and one of them will mail you a summons for each and every violation. And, by the way, we don't need your ID; we have plenty of your information on file. So it looks like you'll be receiving five summonses to district court. And frankly, I don't mind at all being a witness."

"Wait a minute, you and your young sidekick only saw me break four laws, and you never saw me fishing!"

"Nope—you're right, we never saw you fishing, but for now fishing isn't the other violation I am talking about. Your canoe isn't registered to have a motor. According to my calculations, that makes five infractions. When I get to camp I am going to contact Warden Farrar by two-way radio and ask him to meet you at the put-in and give you the invitations to court. If Farrar is busy, then you'll be hearing from us. Nevertheless, you will be hearing!" Turning pale, George said nervously "Last year Farrar gave me a talkin' to and I don't need another." Then once again turning mean, George narrowed his eyes and stared fire at Dalt and said, "Mister— you've just made yourself an enemy!" With that George threw his power saw into the bow of his canoe; jumped in, and headed upstream hurrying to get back to his truck before the game warden showed up.

As George pulled away from shore Dalton called, "By the way, George, where is your personal flotation device [lifejacket], you know they're required?"

"Never carry one 'cause there's no need for 'em. The bulky things just get in the way."

"I oughter let u go without one, but then you'd be illegal about that too—so take this." And with that Dalton grabbed a spare orange lifejacket from the top of their gear and threw it onto the floor of George's canoe, where the vest remained untouched. Dalton followed the loan of the life vest with, "and don't start that motor either or you'll have a sixth summons—which means you'd be spending most of your summer in court."

Ignoring the buoyancy jacket, George grabbed his paddle and propelled his canoe towards the inlet. Jim thought that he could see the air turn blue around George's head as the man uttered curses that were politely carried away by the wind.

CHAPTER XX

Watching the mischief maker until he was out of sight, Dalton and Jim returned to their canoe, and paddled across the lake towards the dock and ranger's cabin.

Pulling up dockside Jim stood on the wharf and appraised the expanse of the lake while Dalton tied up and unloaded their gear. Once all of their equipment was sitting on the dock, each man grabbed a pack and followed the waving flag of Misty's tail, up a wooden ramp, over a familiar rock-strewn path to a building tucked in the woods. Hidden from view of the lake, Jim thought, *the structure looks to be the perfect view point for wardens to watch sports who would be unaware of any valiance by the local garde-chasse.*

At the end of the trail sat a brown-stained, cedar-shingled, framed structure that looked old enough to have been built in the 1940s. Along the front of the camp a screened-in porch invited them to enter. On the roof, held in place by a steel tripod, Jim saw a ten foot section of three-quarter inch steel pipe reaching for the sky. On top of this pipe sat a four-pronged radio antenna patiently waiting for communication that might be received or transmitted through brass rods.

Stepping onto log stairs the two men opened an outside screen door, and walked across the porch and through an interior entry. Passing by the inside planked door, Jim observed, *I do believe that the entry had been made out of wood thick enough to keep out the biggest bear.* Inside, Jim noticed there were three rooms and, despite the building appearing small on the outside, the interior of the camp was spacious and well appointed. Two water buckets sat next to a white sink on a tile-covered counter—the pails served as a reminder that occupants had to lug their wash water from the lake. A propane stove, refrigerator, and gas lights were the only other modern conveniences.

At the back of the camp were two small rooms, each with two twin bunk beds to accommodate a total of four people. Between the bedrooms sat a small woodstove for cold nights. Sliding windows on all four walls ensured a fresh breeze could be enjoyed on hot evenings.

There was a homemade four-foot by three-foot table with four folding gray steel chairs for comfort. To the left of the refrigerator and against the wall, a hardwood stand was positioned to hold the state's 10-watt, two-way radio. An insulated black cable led from the radio set to the antenna on the roof. This communication was used for important messages and emergency situations—and served as the occupants' only connection to the outside world.

Feeling the call of nature, Jim was pointed toward the outhouse, or as his dad used to call the latrine, a pit privy. Opening the entrance to the outside toilet, Jim saw several notes written on the inside of the door. In bold, black letters from a magic marker one writer had scribed, "Everybody cheer because the boys from Greenville are here." And there were other comments that made references to ingesting some bad food. "Scott Young had an upset stomach, Oct. 1, 1970" and then according to more script, "On the night of Sept. 22, 1971 Tommy Simpson spent more time in the privy than in his bed."

Returning to camp, just to be on the safe side Jim asked, "So do we drink the water from the lake?"

"Not really. The lake water is ok for dishes and such and may be ok to consume, but rather than take a chance we'll get our drinking water from the spring to the right of the Ledges Campsite; the water there is very cold and safe to ingest."

Dalton then picked up a handwritten note he found

tucked under a small rock on the table and read out loud:

"Hi Dalton, Thanks for covering for me. I hope that I won't be gone more than a couple of weeks. There is food in the refrigerator. You would be doing me a favor if you would eat the grub in the freezer too. I'll be bringing fresh supplies when I come back. There is gas and oil for the canoe in the shed, along with my chainsaw in case there is a windstorm. There should be plenty of LP gas in the propane bottles, but there is a spare tank in the shed as well, if you need it.

"I understand that there are to be a number of parties coming onto the lake. Several scout troops have been through and more are on their way. The forest is awful dry so watch for unattended fires or lightning strikes. Recently, we've had a number of reports about smoke from a forest fire, but the residue is from a wildfire in Quebec, so it shouldn't be a worry.

"There are a couple of things you should watch for: our friend George has been in quite a lot. Not sure what he is up to but he is here frequently. You should keep an eye on the ice caves, lots of folks have been exploring the underground and many claimed to have heard strange sounds.

Good luck, please leave me a report of how things go for you. The Chamberlain Bridge ranger or supervisor Leigh can help if you need anything. Thanks for helping out—I know the lake is in good hands.

Sincerely,

Jon

That night a light wind whispered through the branches of a nearby pine while the call of a loon heralded a welcome to our world—Jim dreamt.

He is sitting on a grass bank looking at the back wall of a building under construction. The structure is getting quite tall and blocks any view of the water. The assembly has cutouts for windows and doors but none are installed. One rafter has been nailed in place and that truss indicates that a sharp-pitched roof is required. Jim is dressed in a white t-shirt, green cotton pants, a forest green trail cap, and L.L. Bean boots. He is wearing insect repellent to keep the horse flies at bay.

Jim doesn't know where he is, or why the building is there. But it looks like it will be a nice spot to visit—someday.

*****

Dalton and Jim spent the next several days accomplishing an endless amount of chores including checking people that came and went from the nine tent sites (which Dalton reminded could accommodate 14 parties). They cleared brush from the fire tower trail from the lakeshore to the top of Allagash Mountain. The two workers canoed downstream to remove sweepers from the stream as well as clean and check the campsite at Little Allagash Falls. Using a chainsaw they removed blow downs from the portage trail that led to Round Pond. After removing the brush, the two walked the nearby state property line to inspect the progress of jobbers harvesting wood in the nearby One-Mile [harvesting] Zone.

Once back on the lake, Dalton's and Jim's duties also included registering parties that arrived from Johnson Pond, raking campsites, and the inglorious task of keeping the outhouses clean. The two spent several days checking the state's property line where they replaced rotted corner posts as needed and dozens of other labor-intensive chores.

Mixed in with the physical work was the daily education of interpreting the area to the lake's visitors, enforcing regulations, fighting forest fires, conducting search and rescue, or providing ordinary first aid. Jim soon learned that just because they headed out in one direction in the morning, didn't mean they would be returning the same way *and not necessarily before dark either.* They always carried their emergency packs that included a two-way radio, spare rations, a first aid kit, rain coats, thermal blanket, and flashlights. Misty spent her days chasing squirrels, sitting in the middle of the canoe, smelling the air, and welcoming anyone who came by.

On the days that they were able to eat supper at a reasonable time, the duo would spend the last hour of daylight fishing for squaretails, lake trout, or whitefish. Anytime they caught a big brookie, Dalton would remind, "when you cook it up, don't forget about the 'cheek meat.' It's about the size of a quarter and is the tenderloin meat of the brook trout."

Then before bed, Dalton would regale Jim with the history of the area, offering hints about people and animals that Jim could expect to face, if he were ever to be left in here alone. There wasn't any mention of the heirloom until one night when Dalton pulled out a cardboard box full of historical information about the north woods.

Included in the collection was a set of travel books titled "In the Maine Woods." Noticing the series, Jim immediately picked up a copy and asked, what are these? I've never seen this type of book before."

So Dalton explained. "In the early 1900s the Bangor and Aroostook Railroad published these books to promote the Maine outdoors. The logs were very popular when first distributed and hardcover copies quickly had become collector's items." At a glance, Jim could see that the earliest journal in the set was dated 1905 and every edition was in the collection right up to the year 1957. And in its own place in the box, inside a protective covering was an official appearing document titled *Surveying an Underground Natural Resource—The Allagash Ice Caves by Melissa Hendrickson.*

This report Dalton handed directly to Jim and said, "This might be of interest. Let me know when you're done with it," and with that Dalton and Misty shuffled off to bed. Lying in his bunk and reading by flashlight, Jim learned that the Ice Caves were first discovered late one wintery day in 1897. The entrance to the cavern was found quite by accident and occurred after two Greenville lumberjacks cut a large spruce that was nearby the cave. The removal of the tree exposed the opening to the underground, and thinking that the cavity was a bear's den and *that perhaps fresh meat would be a welcome change from camp food*, they used a small spruce tree as a ladder and climbed about 15 feet down the branched log, where the men found a large room.

Running out of sunlight they returned the next day and discovered that the first room was 50 feet across and covered with Little Brown Bats, with many of the flying mammals hanging from the rock ceiling in large clusters. The lumbermen eventually dropped down into a second room where there was a short passage into a third room. From there they found a small crack in the rock wall where there was a fourth room with an entrance so narrow, only a small man could enter. After exploring the cave completely, they left without any bear meat and, because of the harsh winter working conditions, their memories of the discovery soon faded.

Absorbing the report, Jim fell asleep reminding himself, *I've got to remember to ask more about this geological formation in the morning.*

Over breakfast Dalton explained that fissures had

always been considered mysterious and unique—a place where people have explored the intricate chambers and passageways for years. Jim also told DJ about a picture he had found in a 1927 edition of the B&A's "In the Maine Woods." The photograph portrayed three people who had carried a camera the 180 feet in elevation from the cove on the lake, to the entrance of the Caves, and then traversed 75 feet down into the ground to make a record of their adventure. Jim also read that due to the nature of the name "Ice Caves" fisherman and others often went there in search for chunks of ice to help preserve the food in their coolers.

ENTRANCE TO THE ICE CAVES, ALLAGASH LAKE. (T. CAVERLY PHOTO.)

"And then there were the peculiar occurrences. Sometime people let their imagination run away and believed the ground to be breathing when they felt air exhaled from the upper and lower entrances. "It was," as some described, "as if the cave had become, through magic, a living entity.""

"But," Dalt explained, "The exhaling of vapors were really caused by a chimney and reverse chimney effect by two entrances.

"You see inside the caves the air has an average year round temperature of 39°F. This constant allows the cooler heavier air current to flow out of the lower entrance in the summer and the lighter warmer air to escape out the upper entrance during the winter. (Ibid 1).

"And then there were the," here Dalton paused for a moment for effect as he took a sip of coffee, "unexplainable clamors that seem to only occur at night."

"Noises?" Jim questioned.

Nodding yes DJ answered "every once in a while people think they hear strange sounds emitting from the cavities below."

"What kind of noises?"

"Well, the accounts vary. Some report hearing an

echo type of singing; sometimes folks hear a rhythmic chant. Mind you, I've never heard the sounds myself, but the stories are similar to the tales about UFOs and mountain lions which have floated around this country for years. None of the rumors have ever been substantiated, but never-the-less those claims still turn up from time to time.

"I always figured it was the squeak of bats that folks were hearing. You see the cave is home to the Little Brown Bat and the Northern Long Eared Bat—and if they get excited the little critters can be quite harmonious." Here Dalton smiled and continued, "I am not really a bat kind of guy, but I do appreciate the over 600 mosquitoes the little guys will eat an hour. But then there was the incident your grandfather had with Ley Lines …"

Stopping in mid-speech, Dalton looked at Misty who had suddenly sat up, growled, and stared at the porch door. Listening, the two men soon understood what had captured the dog's attention; it was the drone of an aircraft circling low over the camp. Jumping up from the kitchen table, Dalton and Jim hurried onto the porch where they scanned the lake for any signs of trouble.

Immediately the two men saw a blue Cessna floatplane dip to make a quick bank to the right and drop low over the trees to make an abrupt landing on the lake; about 100 feet in front of the ranger's dock. These unexpected visitors interrupted any chance that Jim had to ask questions about the strange noises, to inquire about the mysterious heirloom, or to find out about his grandfather's experiences.

CHAPTER XXI

Opening the screen door of the porch, Dalton ran down the path to the lake with Jim and Misty following close behind. Arriving on the dock at the same time the three ran saw the plane taxiing across the water, ever so slowly towards the ranger's wharf. Once the pilot was within drifting range of the float, he cut his engine, climbed out the left door of the plane, and stood on the pontoon; allowing the momentum of the craft to bring him to the dock. Looking in through the windows of the plane, Jim saw three passengers whose faces were as white as ghosts.

Standing on the tie-up, Dalton grabbed the wing of the plane, brought it to a full stop and asked "Are you ok? What in the world happened? I've never seen you come down so fast!"

Red faced from embarrassment, the airman said, "Do you remember the time when you loaned a life preserver to some of my sports?"

"Yes, reckon I do, but that was a while back."

"I know, but this morning I landed at Johnson to pick them up for a return flight to Greenville. Just as we took off from the pond the people remembered the preserver and asked if we could return the vest to you on our flight over. I said sure. So we circled the cabin and pushed the life jacket out the side window. Wouldn't you know the wind grabbed the life preserver and carried it into the plane's horizontal stabilizer and left side elevator, where the dang thing hung, freezing the control in landing mode. Before I knew it, we were on the lake.

"I apologize for coming in, because I know planes aren't allowed to land here. But I really didn't have much choice in the matter."

Dalton replied, "That's fine, I know accidents happen. I am just glad no one was hurt. There would have been an awful lot of paperwork for me to fill out."

Grinning at Dalton's attempt to make light of a near-death experience; the pilot walked back along the float, grabbed the orange preserver from the tail section of the aircraft, tossed it to Jim, and said, "Guess we'll be on our way, again. If you are ever in town, stop in for coffee." With that the airman climbed inside the craft, started the plane, and began his taxi with the three passengers offering a relieved wave at the two men and dog watching from the dock.

"By the way," the pilot hollered out his window, "there looks to be another orange life preserver floating in the back water by the inlet. Guess it fell out of someone's canoe."

Waving at the pilot to indicate he heard, Dalton turned to Jim and with a twisted grin said, "I'll bet dollars to donuts that's the jacket I gave to George. He probably threw it overboard as soon as he was out of sight."

With the emergency interrupting their conversation, Dalton said "Let's go pick up the flotation device, then we'll head down to the Carry Trail to see if anyone has portaged over from Round Pond."

*****

With the demands of the day, the morning's discussion was soon forgotten. Dalton continued his role of teacher and Jim gladly accepted his current occupation of student. By the end of the week, Jim had absorbed all that Dalton could teach. He learned about the logging history of the area: the iron ring sunk into the ledge island east of Sandy Point, the wing dam at the Outlet, the remains of an older dam by the first set of rapids on the lower Allagash Stream, and more.

Then Jim discovered that during the late 1950s into the early 1960s there were the tent camps that dotted the landscape around the lake. One camp located east of the Carry Trail was

- 154 -

constructed by pilot Elmer Wilson for use by Frank and Nina Sawyer of Island Falls.

NINA SAWYER CAMP NEAR CARRY TRAIL, ALLAGASH LAKE 1963.

NINA SAWYER PHOTO. (T. CAVERLY COLLECTION.)

There were also several other camps about the same time. Folsom's Flying Service had a base camp behind Five Islands, and another out camp was constructed in the Cove Campsite. There was still another seasonal structure near the Ice Caves.

FOREST FRENZY
A NEWSLETTER FROM THE ALLAGASH WOODS
A SPECIAL REPORT FOR
"THE NORTH WOODS GAZETTE"

By Tom Holt

Vol. 14, July 1979

THE MYSTERY OF THE WOODEN BOX

Since those many years ago when I first wrote about my experiences and those folks who call the woods home; I have hiked countless paths, canoed numerous trails, and experienced so many adventures in the Allagash woods; that I am not sure enough ink exists to print all of the encounters.

So it is with humility that I must present this, dear reader, as my last installment of stories from the North Country. I have decided to hang up my typewriter and live full-time as a caretaker at a set of camps, not far from Allagash

Lake. My days from here on out will be spent fishing, swatting blackflies, repairing buildings, hunting, exploring old features, discovering new countryside, and canoeing cold water streams; where I prefer to think no one has gone before.

Rest assured I will be easy to find, hard to disagree with, and that a pot of coffee will always "be on the back burner" to encourage conversation. Here is my final story and I hope you enjoy.

It began as many days do in the woods, as a calm morning on Allagash Lake. I had spent the night before with the Waterway ranger and over a supper of marinated togue, canned fiddleheads, oven baked potatoes, and biscuits slathered with creamery butter; we had resolved many of the world's issues. (If we could only get the politicians to spend such an evening, perhaps they could do the same.) The editor had assigned me to spend several days patrolling with the ranger and learn firsthand what life was like for these stalwarts of the forest.

In amidst our conversation about wildlife behavior, secret fishing spots, odd antics by the travelers, we discussed the area's history. During our exchange it came up that at one time several tent-camps had been spread around the shore of the lake. These had generally been built by Folsom's Flying Service for use as "out-camps." One such location was the Cove Campsite, just around the bend from the ranger's station.

The ranger had indicated that he'd heard there was still an old supply box, once used by the flying service, that could be located near that site; the ranger had looked for the chest but never found it. I asked if we could give it another try and so off we went. Now these wooden boxes, as I understand, were about four foot in length, three feet wide, and two feet tall. A hinged cover provided protection to the contents and prevented varmints from getting inside. In these boxes guides would stockpile such things as frying pans, enamel bakeware, Coleman stoves and fuel, dish soap, utensils; or anything else that could be used during the next visit.

Pulling up to the Cove Campsite in our canoe we noticed a tent and a person standing near the picnic table. The ranger seemed to know the individual as someone who visited often. So in everyday conversation the ranger asked if the camper had ever seen the old supply box which was thought to be nearby. The man said that they had found the container just that morning. I asked if he could show us and he indicated that his father was asleep in the tent and certainly would want to go as well. The man asked us if we could come back in an hour so the father can accompany us? The ranger agreed we could come back, so he and I headed off to clean campsites, check permits, and to verify that the eggs of a Bonaparte's Gull had indeed hatched.

Two hours later we return to the Cove Campsite, as requested. On our inquiry we learned that the man's dad was still asleep, but if we would take our guide around to the landing around the point in our canoe he would lead us to the container. With three people in our water vehicle, we reached the other side at some distance from the campsite and followed our guide into the woods. He took great care to lead us over only the highest blowdowns, through the thickest raspberry bushes, and into the soggiest wetlands where we swatted at clouds of very hungry blackflies.

After stumbling for a considerable distance he turned us back towards the lake, saying we had walked too far. By this time, as it was also quite hot, we were quite anxious to find the elusive chest. At the same instant that we saw the blue of the lake, the ranger spied the chest. He was so excited to achieve this long sought-after goal, that he immediately started hollering, "The box, the box, I can see the box!" And he began jumping over horizontal logs hurrying to the prize.

What we didn't know was that the father, who was alleged to have been sleeping, had quietly snuck over to the container, climbed inside, and closed the cover.

When the ranger reached the wooden chest, still quite excited, he immediately raised the lid to peer inside. When he opened the top, the old man roared and stood up like he was a very grumpy bear. Not expecting the box to be occupied, the ranger hollered words too explicit for me to print, and slammed the lid down.

The cover banged to a shut, and howls of muffled laughter came from inside the box and gales of glee were heard from the son throughout the forest. Scared almost into a heart attack, it took some time for the ranger to appreciate the humor of the situation.

But he has now recovered and I am pleased to report the old supply box is alive and well, and waiting to be once again discovered.

Such is everyday life in the Maine woods.

WOODS BOX

Each night Jim would read from the collected works that had been saved in the cardboard box and he soon found that the box contained a treasure trove of north woods history. One of the magazines he found especially interesting was an outdoor publication that explained the history of the first fire tower on Allagash Mountain.   Built in 1916 the tower was constructed out of logs and stood a lofty 20 feet high. During the first year of operation watchman Eldridge G. Jones of Bangor, spotted four forest fires from the new lookout. That same year a log cabin to house the watchman was built halfway up the trail.

After the structures were completed Allagash Mountain tower needed to be able to communicate with nearby Soper Mountain tower. So in the same year of construction of the tower, a phone line was run from Allagash tower to the Soper Mountain tower; over a trail that had been previously brushed out in 1915—a distance of 36 miles to the east.***2

In 1924, the Allagash Mountain log tower was replaced with a 27-foot steel structure, and in 1948 the old log camp on the trail was replaced by a building near the lake so the watchman could be resupplied by boat or plane. (Ibid 2)

2. History as supplied by the Forest Fire Lookout Association-Maine Chapter.)

1918 ALLAGASH MOUNTAIN WATCHMAN'S CAMP.

(PHOTOGRAPH COURTESY OF FOREST FIRE LOOKOUT ASS'N..

MAINE CHAPTER.)

Jim also read about the antics of local wildlife, deer, moose, partridge, loons, and the time when a bear became annoyed by a particular campsite sign. It had happened one spring when a new sign had been installed at the Cove Campsite. The marker had been in place for only a short time when a black bear clawed the face of the sign. The damaged symbol was replaced and the bear scored into the wood logo a second time. After the animal damaged a third sign the state decided that the bear had won and left the scratched signpost in place.

Jim learned there was tons of native wildlife that depended on the lake for their sustenance. He thought, *gosh if I wrote down every kind of flora and fauna we saw, the list would be longer than both our arms.* There were the Bonaparte's Gull and Arctic Terns that lived on the lake, the hardy wood frog, Stone Fly nymphs, beavers, ospreys, eagles, great blue herons, the Barred and Great Horned owls, just to name a few. Geologically there were the odd-shaped 400-million-year-old volcanic outcrops of pillow lava and the old scratches in the lakeshore ledges. Scrapes caused 12,000 years ago by glaciers that proved that giant blocks of ice had once gouged the countryside. And then there were the sweet, wild sugar plum bushes that grew on some of the islands.

But there were also sad occasions such as drowning's— reading about the accidents is when Jim realized just how quickly the lake could turn deadly. For example, in the fall of 1967, a forest warden died off Sandy Point on the north end of the lake. The man had been cleaning the campsite when his watercraft boat drifted off. The fellow tried to swim after the runaway boat, but didn't make it.

Warden's Body Found In Remote Maine Lake

GREENVILLE — Searchers recovered the body Tuesday of a forest warden who has been missing at Allagash Lake since Oct. 15 and a Piscataquis County medical examiner ruled that death was due to accidental drowning.

The body of Alton Buzzell, 45, of Lincoln was located about 11:40 a.m. during dragging operations on the deep lake in the northwest corner of Piscataquis County, about 60 miles north of Greenville.

Deputy Sheriff Earl Tukey of Milo said he and Deputy Sheriff Maurice Sleeper, also of Milo, were using grapples when they caught the body. Tukey said charts indicated the water was about 60 feet deep at the point.

The officer said the body was located about 125 yards off shore in a straight line from where the man's tracks had led into the water.

Authorities launched a search for Buzzell, who had been a summer fire tower lookout on Allagash Mountain, on Oct. 17 after he failed to check in by radio. His last contact was Oct. 15 when he had used a Maine Forest Service radio to say he was going to check campsites in the area.

Searchers subsequently found a pile of his clothing on a beach and they theorized he had gone into the water in an effort to retrieve his boat which had drifted away.

The craft was subsequently found some distance away on the lake.

Also conducting dragging operations on the lake Tuesday were three Forest Service personnel.

Dr. Norman Nickerson of Greenville, the medical examiner who was flown to the scene, said the body had been flown to Lincoln.

Then Jim learned of another tragedy that occurred in 1977. At the time the Department of Parks and Recreation was considering a policy to require the Allagash Lake ranger to paddle (rather than motor) his 20-foot aluminum canoe around the 4,000-acre lake during his routine patrol. That spring, just after ice out, and before the administrators had made their final decision, the ranger was instructed to leave the lake and attend a spring meeting at the headquarters on Umsaskis Lake.

While the patrolman was away, the weather turned deadly. At the time there was a party of four camped in the Cove Campsite, and three of the members decided to go fishing. Piling into one canoe they headed out for a day on the water.

When the three fishermen didn't return, the fourth member of the party paddled to the fire warden's camp—broke in and used a two-way radio to call for help. A search plane was dispatched and the three men were found floating face down in the water not too far from the Five Islands on the southeast side of the lake. All were wearing their lifejackets and it was suspected that their deaths were caused by hypothermia. Here Dalton emphasized, "Remember, survival in the woods is only as safe as you are careful, observant, and prepared."

*****

The beginning of the next week, being Sunday, Jim was spending the dawn hours of the morning relaxed on the dock, and watching the sun warm the eastern sky. Dalton brought him a cup of coffee and said, "Did I tell you about the time I went swimming with all my clothes on?"

"Don't think so ... why would you do that?"

Handing the coffee to Jim, the man stared at the water and said "well it happened late one afternoon on a very hot day. I'd come down to the dock to get a bucket of water for dishes. When I stepped onto the wharf, I heard a noise to my left and when I turned, there were two women, completely naked, paddling by. I stared at them so bad that I kept on walking, right off the dock into the lake. I went right down and "and shut the door." When I resurfaced, I could hear the girls giggling. I think I was more embarrassed about the ladies' lack of clothes than the girls themselves." Smiling, Dalton reflected for a moment about the escapade and then said more seriously.

"Guess it's time we had a talk."

"Sure," Jim replied as he reached for the steaming mug.

"Well, you're one of the quickest learners I've ever seen, and I think you've absorbed about all I can share. How would you like to work here for a few days?"

"Guess I'm not sure what you mean?"

"I've got a doctor's appointment tomorrow, and I'd like to leave this afternoon to get ready for it. You've got enough food to last a few more days and if you wanna stay; I'll clear it with the boss. We can sign you up as a volunteer so it will be ok for you to use the canoe and motor—that is if

"You don't mind cleaning a campsite now and then?"

Surprised by this sudden revelation, Jim thought for a moment and replied, "I guess I'd like that.

"Dalton?"

"Yeah?"

"We never did finish that conversation about my grandfather and Ley Lines. I've never heard of these lines—what are they?"

"According to legend, Ley Lines are mythical bands of energy that circle the earth; a type of electric force that can be either positive or negative. For years people have claimed that these bands exist. Look through the box of material and you'll find a newspaper article based on such an alignment right here on Allagash Lake. In fact, it is because of those Ley Lines that your grandfather had the experience he did and they are the reason you're here. Go ahead and read the commentary while I pack, then we'll talk."

Reluctant to leave his front row seat of watching the early dawn, Jim rose to his feet and followed Dalton into the camp. Pulling the file of material off the top bunk in the spare room Jim thumbed through the collection until he found the piece that Dalton had recommended.

FOREST FRENZY

A NEWSLETTER FROM THE ALLAGASH WOODS

A SPECIAL REPORT FOR

"THE NORTH WOODS GAZETTE"

By Tom Holt

Vol. 15, July 1978

LEY LINES

An old trapper once told me that "there are enough real-life adventures in the Maine woods, so stories don't need to be made up" — and in the last few years that I have traveled into the north country, I have certainly found that to be true.

This tale comes directly from a Jim Clark, a man going on in years who has traveled the bush more than anyone I know, and in his words, "I've hiked the breadth of this country — from stem to stern, from low swamp to high ground, from old growth forest to clear cuts."

Speaking with people who know him, I've learned that Jim is well respected. Others have said he is soft in speech, of good humor, and easy to be around. In my brief time of talking with him, I've found that all to be true. This is Mr. Clark's story, as told to me one night sitting around the campfire on the Ledge Campsite after I had asked about his most unusual experience.

"During my years traipsing around these parts, there is one incident that sticks out the most. A few years ago I was having a difficult time at home. Work had been stressful and there wasn't enough money to pay my bills. Because of finances and losing our ability to talk, the wife and I weren't getting along very well. Then we had nosy neighbors who were constantly trying to get me involved in local squabbles. I didn't feel well physically and I was worried about my daughter and her new marriage, after only a year it appeared that the young couple was headed for a divorce. I finally told my wife that I needed to get away for a few days, so I decided to come to Allagash Lake to see my friend Dalton. My wife agreed.

"When I arrived on the lake, I learned Dalton was away on days off, so I set up camp on the Ice Cave Campsite." Here Old Jim pointed a steady finger across the lake and continued, "right over there. I was the only one on this end of the lake so I placed my tent where the evening breeze would keep the blackflies at bay. With enough firewood for the evening, I settled down to listen to the loons and watch the trout feed on a green drake hatch.

"Time had slipped away and as dark approached, I noticed a weather front was coming in from the southeast. A storm coming from this direction isn't unusual, but it was the clouds that seemed peculiar. They weren't low-hanging clouds, but weren't high ones either — right in the middle I'd say.

"As I watched 'em get closer, they seemed to bump and grind against each other, as if the billows were racing to get somewhere. Pretty quick I was covered in a thick fog, couldn't even see the back of my hand. Then I heard a distant rumbling coming from the caves up the hill. Looking towards the sound, I saw a succession of fireflies fly in from the surface of the lake up the hill towards the cavern. Appearing like low-watt Christmas bulbs, the creatures landed on the ground, where the swarm sat in little bug fashion, end to end; blinking their little stomachs on and off; outlining both sides of the trail. Being a curious sort, I followed this illuminated path to the upper entrance of the cave.

"But the lightning bugs didn't stop there. Their light went right down into the cave and oddly enough, when I ducked under the overhanging ledge, I saw that the lichen had oddly grown on the ledge in the exact shape of my initials — JPC. Now I'd been in the cave before and I knew it was about 15 feet down to the first large chamber, but I'd never seen the lettering before.

"Entering without a flashlight, I found this hanging off a piece of tree root." Here Jim pulled a ribbon from around his neck that had an 1838 Liberty copper penny attached.

"It was clear that a hole had been drilled along the top of the one cent coinage to allow for the money to be worn like a necklace. Perhaps the oddest thing was that, on the obverse of the penny, someone had stamped the same letters as are in my initials — JPC.

"At the time I thought it odd to discover such a find, but finally figured the necklace had been lost by a previous hiker, and the similarity of the letters was just a coincidence.

"Well as I climbed deeper I started hearing strange sounds. Like gunfire and people hollering, as if some sort of battle was going on. In front of me, on a moist wall, I saw the image of a bearded man wearing a soldier's blue uniform. And he was wearing a coin like the one I had found — around his neck in today's military fashion of a dog tag. Another soldier dressed in gray aimed a rifle point blank at him and pulled the trigger. The gun misfired and the Union soldier tackled him.

"That scene faded and another one appeared. This scene was one of two woodcutters who were using double-bitted axes to fell trees. The second lumberjack didn't see the first cutter and he felled a huge pine that was headed towards the first man—certain to cause immediate death. Suddenly a gust of north wind came out of nowhere and blew the pine off course, saving the woodcutter's life.

"I heard more noise below and the lightning bugs now lit the path down to a second chamber. Following the illumination, I entered a smaller space and on the walls of this fissure a scene flickered before me as before. This time, the person flashing across the smooth rock screen was me. I was snowshoeing through a deep, fresh powder of snow. Then the laces of my right snowshoe broke and I was walking with only a snowshoe on my left foot. With every step my right foot was sinking about 24 inches in the snow while my left foot, still wearing the snowshoe, was staying on the white surface. I could see that I was getting tired. Out of nowhere a Native American stepped from around a large spruce. He handed me a piece of spruce limb with sinew. I was able to use this dried animal tendon as cordage to tie the bough onto my boot. The makeshift snowshoe wasn't great, but it was better than nothing—I was able to continue walking without sinking so deep.

"Then that scene faded and the path once again illuminated down to a third chamber. A young man appeared in the shadows on the wall, and he appeared to be under some sort of grief — staring at a casket.

"This time there was a new person being portrayed on the wall. The image could be a younger me, but I don't think it was me because of the old style clothing he was wearing. It was spring, there was snow along the shore and the young man was in a canoe, crossing a lake. The wind came up and he was in danger of capsizing. The intensity of the wind increased, and there were trees toppling all around the lake. The person tipped over and disappeared under the swells of cold water. The canoe filled with water and became partly submerged. The odd thing with all of this was that in the first two scenes the man was wearing a necklace such as the one I have on. The boy, who went over in the canoe, wasn't.

"Once again the images faded and a path took me down once again to a fourth cavity. The opening was very narrow; I could barely squeeze through. On the wall there I saw a young man who appeared to be very worried. Then a woman appeared and brought a smile to his otherwise taunt features. In another frame, the man is excited to receive the news about the birth of a new baby boy. In this image, a distance voice says they plan to call the boy Jim.

"After this last vision, I could see the lights along

the path beginning to fade. Not having my flashlight, I decided to leave before I lost the light by the fireflies. I wore the necklace out of the cave, planning to turn it into the ranger when he returned. The next day I was fishing out on the lake, when a sudden wind came up. I felt my canoe starting to fill up with water. There wasn't anyone on the lake and the gusts became so strong that trees were being uprooted.

"Then I saw a calm water pathway open up to the shore, back to my campsite. Once on shore, the forest was in complete upheaval—except for where I was standing. The storm lasted most of the evening blowing out by the following morning. I wore the necklace home and for several years after. I always planned to return it, and still do."

By now, the coals from the campfire had died and tired from a long day and with so much to think about, we turned in.

Such is everyday life in the Maine woods.

PART IV

"There is a place where the windows of an abandoned trapper's camp peek under low-hanging branches, watching and waiting for its owner to return."

CHAPTER XXII

Finished with the document, Jim placed the newspaper on the kitchen table. Doubting the authenticity of such a story he couldn't help but realize. *Oh my gosh! This must have been written about my grandfather discovering an amulet. A talisman—a charm that allowed him to view the past and look into the future. This report can't be real, or can it? But who were all the people he saw?*

"Have you read all of it?" Dalton inquired.

"Yes," Jim replied.

"What do ya think?"

"Is the story true?" Jim asked, every fiber of his being was saying that it wasn't possible.

"Well, I think it must be. At least your grandfather claimed every word was real.

"True to his word—old Jim did return to drape the penny necklace over that old tree root, where he originally found. That is when his bad lucked started though. It wasn't long after your gramps took off the good luck piece that he was diagnosed with cancer. The disease overtook Old Jim quickly and rapidly made the man weak. But even so Old Jim made one final trip in to spend a night with me at camp. It was then that he told me some of what had happened. But then again, I suspect he never told me everything that he saw that night. Well, he had returned to asked for my help with a letter; the correspondence that brought you here.

"By morning we had finished an acceptable draft and it was time for him to leave. I stood on the dock and watched him settle into the stern of his canoe only to see him turned and say, 'when you see my grandson show him the ropes and tell him about my experience–will you?' 'Guess I can,' I responded, 'but how will I know him?'

"Old Jim thought for a minute and then offered, 'By the phrase, Le moment est venu. In fact, I'll add that to the letter. When you hear a man say, Le moment est venu, say hello to my grandson and don't be surprised if his name is Jim.'

"I watched the old guy paddle upstream straight and proud as he headed towards the future. We talked by phone a couple of times after that, but he died before I ever got the chance to see him again. But you know there was an odd thing about him leaving that coin behind. I don't doubt his word, but after he was gone, I walked up to the entrance of that hole in the ground to look for the good luck piece and the tree root, but never found either. Then again, I always wondered what 'ropes' I was supposed to show you.

"Well young fellow, it's time for me to head up to the truck. Remember what I've told you and if you need help contact Leigh by radio. Remember when you're at camp the call sign is **Allagash Lake** and if you are mobile on the lake, then the call sign is **1703**." The woodsman then commanded, "Into the bow Misty," and the dog jumped to its assigned seat in the front of the canoe and sat down. From her perch, the pet stared back at her master over a left shoulder as if to say ok *I'm ready. By the way I did such a good job obeying don't you think I deserve a biscuit?*

Jim felt alone as he watched the team leave. Partway across the lake, Dalton hollered back to Jim with one more set of instructions, "remember to keep an eye on for George. I should be back in a few days."

*****

What am I going to do now, wondered Jim as he walked slowly back up the trail toward the camp to make coffee and plan the day's activities. With time going faster than he ever imagined it didn't take Jim long to learn that days pass very quickly for someone who lives in the woods.

- 179 -

There was always something to occupy his waking hours; parties stopping at camp to request information about the weather, water levels in the river, or asking him to explain the fishing regulations. Jim sometimes had the unfortunate duty of delivering emergency messages from back home to folks who were on their once in a lifetime adventure in the middle of nowhere. Other times he provided first aid, explained regulations, reported fishing violations to game wardens, battled forest fires. Once he even had to call a plane in to fly out a little boy who had spilled boiling water on his stomach and who had experienced the painful blistering of third-degree burns.

And there was cleaning campsites. Jim enjoyed working on the sites and felt pleased whenever people commended him for taking such good care of his area. *Little do they know I am only a volunteer,* Jim would secretly smile to himself.

A few days later Jim received a radio call:

"1700 to Allagash Lake." Realizing it was the waterway supervisor on the other end of the radio, Jim nervously answered the two-way communication "Go ahead."

"Can you meet me at the Forest watchman's camp this

afternoon? I've got some paperwork for you to sign."

"Yes I can," then Jim remembered the official language of the air waves, he followed with the acknowledgement he understood of "10-4." Jim suspected that the visit had something to do with signing official volunteer forms.

"10-4," the supervisor replied. "See you in a couple of hours."

Motoring down the lake; Jim passed by a projection of ledge that had an odd look about it. Remembering his college geology class, Jim recalled that this was 400-million-year-old sedimentary rock from the Seboomook Group. In the middle of the rock was a distinct weathering pattern where the thick middle layer displayed a variable lime content and over time, residual calcium in the clay material had washed away; leaving an artistic design.

LEDGE OUTCROPPING, EAST SIDE OF ALLAGASH LAKE. (T. CAVERLY PHOTO.)

A short time later Jim tied off the Grumman canoe at the dock reserved for the Maine Forest Service and saw a tall man in uniform walking confidently to towards him. Sticking out his hand in greeting, he said, "Hi Jim, it's nice to finally meet you. I've been hearing some good things about you. And Dalton couldn't say enough about you being a quick learner."

"You must be Leigh." Jim said as he stuck out his hand to shake the extended grasp. "I sure appreciate you allowing me to stay on as a volunteer. I've been learning a lot."

"That's fine Jim, glad you could help us out. But I have

to tell you we can no longer use your services as a volunteer."
With those words Jim felt like he could have been knocked
over with a feather.

CHAPTER XXIII

Leigh's statement weighed heavily on his mind as Jim worried *do I have to leave? But I can't go back to the farm for another several months.*

"That's right, Jim," the supervisor continued while he watched a pained expression creep across the male's face. Feeling bad to upset the young man, the boss continued, "Dalton is under the weather so he won't be coming back right off. He's fine," the supervisor offered as he saw Jim's look of concern "but our friend has to stay in town for a little while longer. In the meantime, I'd like to offer you an opportunity to go to work. We are quite shorthanded and you've earned the opportunity to be hired as an acting capacity. You'd do us a big favor if you could accept the job for a while."

Jim couldn't believe what he was hearing. *He didn't have to leave; at least right off.* But, "what does acting capacity mean?" he asked.

"It's a bureaucratic tool we use to temporarily fill positions in order to have coverage through the busy season. If you agree, you will receive ranger pay, sick leave, and vacation time but that's where the benefits end. It is short-term employment and you won't have any rights to the position. But you will be able to work on the lake, I'd say for at least a couple of months—if you care to?"

Smiling, Jim asked, "Where do I sign?"

When the paperwork was finished, Leigh explained a few more requirements of the job and recorded Jim's clothing sizes in order to provide him with a uniform. Leigh provided Jim with a daily work schedule and with another shake of the hand said, "Welcome aboard, call me if you need anything." Returning to the canoe, Jim started the outboard and smiled all the way back to camp. Motoring by the back side of the Ice Cave landing Jim saw the same canoe he and Dalton had seen when they first entered the lake—a time that seemed like weeks ago.

It was George's canoe, but Jim didn't see the old poacher anywhere around. Landing at his own dock, Jim saw a shadowy figure fade out of sight behind the woodshed of his camp. It was George, and Jim hollered, "Hold it." George stopped in his tracks.

"You still here?" George questioned sharply.

"Yup," said Jim, and then asked, "You need

something?"

"Nope, just stopped off to visit with my old friend Dalton. Know when he'll be back?"

"Guess he won't be. I am working here now."

"That so?" leered George, *looks like I got me a new fellow to break in,* he thought.

"I'll be headed back to my site now, plan on fishing for a few days." Then George walked away saying, "I am sure we'll be seeing quite a lot of each other."

"Looking forward to it," Jim replied. Walking around camp he saw where someone had tried to break the heavy brass padlock of the shed. *Guess George may have been looking for something he could use. Looks like I got back just in time.*

Going inside to make supper; Jim grabbed a baking sheet, opened a canned ham which he placed on the pan. Once the ham was settled in place, he covered the meat with ringlets of pineapple. Jim then put the main portion of the meal in the oven and washed two potatoes and placed them on the baking sheet as well. One of the 'taters' was to be eaten for supper and the other to serve as home fries in the morning. Carrots were cleaned, cut up, and placed in boiling water. Jim also planned to bake biscuits to accompany his feast, but the bread didn't take very long, so building the dough could wait for a bit. Nothing better than maple syrup poured over hot biscuits slathered with butter to complete a square meal as he hungrily thought ahead to dessert.

While waiting for his evening feast to cook, Jim sat at the kitchen table and leafed through a few of the old Bangor and Aroostook Railroad Travel Logs.

*****

In the 1905 edition, Jim saw that the entrance to the Allagash canoe trip was through the Northeast Carry and trippers should plan on paddling 203 miles; depending on whether they intended to pull off the river in Fort Kent or Van Buren. The publication recommended the Dickey Motel in Fort Kent as the place to stay. *Proprietor J. H. McInerney promised to spare no pains to make all advanced arrangements for our guests, and to transfer canoes, baggage, etc. [by rail] for them.*

The 1922 booklet talked about limits on fish and game and indicated that all sports were allowed 2 deer, 10 ducks, 6 woodcock, five partridge, 25 fish or 15 pounds; whichever came first. The cost of a fishing license was an (expensive) $2.15 for a Maine resident, $3.15 for a nonresident and guides charged $6 to $7/day; a price that included canoe, tent, and cooking utensils.

In the 1940 edition Jim noticed that people were allowed 25 fish a day or up to 7½ lbs. But if the last fish caught exceeded the pound limit, then an overage of the amount of weight was allowed. The booklet promised that clients would catch, "Trout that run sizes [so big] that they will make your eyes bulge." People were welcome to order free copies of the booklet(s) by sending $.15 to cover the cost of stamps.

BANGOR AND AROOSTOOK BOOKLET "IN THE MAINE WOODS" SHOWING CANOE ROUTES IN THE NORTH MAINE WOODS IN 1927.

*****

After eating and still not feeling tired, Jim decided to

leaf through his Grandfather's scrapbook. On the very last page, protected between two sheets of sheepskin parchment he found an obituary. But there was more, under the epitaph he found a newspaper commentary about a Maine civil war hero. Wonder why this is in here? He thought. Reading on, Jim was surprised to find his own name in print. The man soon realized why the obituary and article had been treasured for so long.

JAMES PAUL CLARK

BLESSED TO ARRIVE ON THIS EARTH ON

FEBRUARY 2ND 1838

WENT TO BE WITH OUR LORD

NOVEMBER 16TH 1938

James was a devoted husband, father, war hero and a cherished citizen of Cornville, Maine. In his last remaining days, Mr. Clark was surrounded by family with a profusion of beautiful flowers. Everything that could be done to make him comfortable, was done.

In 1861 he enlisted into the 20th Maine to fight the War of the Rebellion and return peace to our fractured nation. While in the Union army he served on Little Round Top at Gettysburg where he was awarded the Medal of Honor for bravery and promoted to the rank of Lieutenant.

After serving in the Grand Army of the Republic, Jim

returned home to run the family farm where he married Sevilla Getchell, and together they raised three children. Much to his grievement, his lovely wife Sevilla passed several years before; being taken to the lord's house by a case of apoplexy.

In 1884 he volunteered to fight a 22,000 acre forest fire in the Mt. Katahdin area at a set of lumbering camps known as "Old City." A fire that burned so hot it was thought by some to have been caused by the supernatural. The flame came from all directions and, in Mr. Clark's words, "the sky rained fire." That experience of extinguishing the blaze to protect the woods helped Jim develop an appreciation for the outdoors. This love of nature caused Jim to take many trips into the Maine woods, where he loved to hunt and fish–often traveling deep into the forest to camp on Allagash Lake.

Jim is survived by a daughter, Pauline and two sons; Irvin and Jim Jr.

A vigil of his body will be held at their home in Cornville for three days. At the end of this period an internment service will be held at the Skowhegan Congregational Church, where the family plans to sing the hymns Rock of Ages and Abide with Me.

The family has already received numerous tender sympathies from a large number of friends.

GETTYSBURG DAILY EXPRESS
JULY 4TH, 1863
WAR HERO RECOGNIZED
MAN SAYS A PENNY SAVED HIS LIFE

In an unusual turn of events, James Clark of Cornville, Maine is a lucky man. On July 2nd Mr. Clark fought at Gettysburg in the battle of Little Round Top. Clark was with the 20th Maine during Maine's legendary charge by Hood's Alabama Brigade. Clark was the last soldier posted in the single file line of the Union's left flank when he heard orders, "To refuse the line."

It was in the heat of the day when the 15th Alabama made two charges towards our brave lads. Col. Chamberlain knew that his men were out of ammunition; so he commanded fixed bayonets. The soldiers were then ordered to conduct a right-wheel maneuver, with Clark's end of the line swinging downhill like an open door. The unusual maneuver was so successful, the confederates' charge was halted and a good portion of the enemy captured.

When I spoke with the soldier about his heroism, Mr. Clark credited his life to an 1838 braided hair Liberty penny that he wore about his neck. Showing me the coin, I saw that a hole had been drilled through the cent piece to allow the penny to be worn as a necklet. The coinage was stamped with the letters JPC so the currency could be used to identify James in the event of his death.

Mr. Clark, born at his Cornville home in 1838, was given this coin by his grandfather Joseph Sanborn. Mr. Sanborn was well known as the seventh son of a seventh son.***

Lt. Joseph Danborn of Sanbornton, N.H.
(Photograph from T. Caverly collection)

***Author's note:** Since the dawn of time it has been thought that the seventh son of a seventh son held mystical, super natural talents that included such skills as a healer. It was thought that such a person had second sight and could foresee events. In order for a seventh son of a seventh son to enjoy these magical gifts, there had to be a direct line of sons without any of the family births being interrupted by the delivery of a daughter. (www. mystical-www.co.uk on line)*

As Mr. Clark grew into manhood, he learned that the circle of the coin was good luck and it was a sign of wholeness, perfection, and eternity. He was also told that if he wore the pendant with the head out, the currency would bring power and protect him from harm. The copper, minted in Philadelphia, our nation's cradle of liberty and home of independence; has had its lucky nature enhanced by those same principles which has made our country great. Mr. Clark has been wearing the token for years.

During the heat of battle, Mr. Clark's rifle was empty when the order came to charge. He was only partway down the hill during the attack when a confederate soldier stepped in front of our hero and pulled the trigger of a .58 caliber Mississippi rifle, aiming at him point blank. The gun refused to fire. The confederate soldier then pulled a .44 Kerrs patent revolver and aimed directly at Mr. Clark's head. Once again the gun misfired. Mr. Clark took the advantage of the situation and captured his opponent.

According to substantiated reports, there have been several occasions during the war where others have been killed or wounded, but Mr. Clark remained untouched.

1838 Braided Liberty copper penny.

When asked about his plans after the war, Mr. Clark says he will return to his farm, explore Maine and he designs to share this talisman with his family.

God speed Mr. Clark; god speed. And thank you!

*****

It was now clear to Jim what he was expected to find. But he still wasn't sure how, why, even where it was. Guess I'll just have to wait for a sign. Hope I don't have to wait too long.

That night Jim had another dream;

As in the other visions, Jim is standing on a gravel driveway. A small portion of a blue lake can be seen off to his left. A brand-new log cabin is blocking part of his view. The kitchen door of the lodge is open and Jim walks in, followed closely by a golden retriever. He sees that the building is completely furnished and a fieldstone fireplace complements a huge living room. Two picture windows offer a vista of the surrounding area. Jim sees that a worker is installing electrical outlets that are connected to a generator in a rounded log outbuilding. And there are bedrooms, enough sleeping arrangements to accommodate a complement of men and women.

The worker turns and hands Jim a set of keys and beams, "Everything is finished and it's all yours."

CHAPTER XXIV

Rising early the next morning, Jim walked down to the dock for a morning swim when he noticed George already paddling down the lake, headed east, towards the outlet. Watching through his field glasses, Jim could see a fishing rod with a bobber hanging from the tip of the fishing line stored in the bow of the canoe. *Guess George has gone fishing. I'll pay him a surprise visit in a bit to see if he is using worms illegally.*

An hour later, Jim arrived at the Outlet Campsite to look for George; the new ranger planned to speak with the old fellow about the damage to the woodshed. But neither the man nor his canoe could be found. *That's odd*, Jim thought. *I could have sworn I saw him down here. Hum—wonder what he is up to?*

Jim never saw George again that day and found out later that the poacher had returned late, actually after dark, to the Ice Cave Campsite.

*****

A week later Jim awoke to a ruckus coming from the east end of the lake. In the deep woods of Maine it wasn't uncommon to hear wildlife having conversations, but today the banter seemed to be a bit early and very, very agitated.

The man threw back the bed sheet and sat up on the edge of the narrow bunk. Pulling his folded, uniform pants from their overnight perch on the back of a folding chair, he stood up and slid into the forest green slacks one leg at a time. Jim buckled a wide, black leather belt to hold the pants in place, and then he sat back down onto the bunk. Seated he pulled on wool socks and stuck his feet into his footwear of preference; the L.L. Bean Hunting shoe. Jim liked that boot because it kept his feet the driest (and they had been his grandfather's boots). Dry footwear was very important for someone who spent their life working around water.

It had been hot all evening so before *hitting the hay* as his grandfather had called going to bed; the ranger had left the interior door open that led to the screened-in porch. It was a futile attempt for the small cabin to capture as much of a cross breeze as possible. The night before Jim had felt exhausted so when he went to bed, he only covered up with a thin cotton sheet.

Once his feet were dressed he walked through the kitchen of the cabin towards the screen door. From a coat hook by the kitchen door he grabbed his uniform shirt, outfitted with a ranger badge, name tag, and Department of Conservation patches on both shoulders. Double checking, Jim made sure that his field compass was secure in its assigned location of the shirt's right pocket.

Placing the ranger cap onto his head with the visor pulled over his eyes, he could now be recognized as a person to be in charge of a situation; if he needed to be.

Without even a thought he grabbed the strap of his field glasses that always hung on a nail on the screened porch. Ready for the day, the man in uniform strode down the path towards the dock. Walking quickly, a light perspiration beaded on his forehead, indicating that the temperature hadn't cooled much during the night. On the north end of the dock, the state's 20-foot Grumman patrol canoe sat easy in the water, waiting for its day's assignment.

An eight-horse, Mercury outboard motor hung off the left side of the double-ended craft's stern. The outboard motor's red gas tank was full because in the short time Jim had been on the lake, he had learned that you just never knew when an emergency might come to call, and he wanted or was it he needed, to be ready.

Standing on the 10-foot by 20-foot dock and looking

over the water towards the Outlet Campsite, the inland sea was dead calm. Pea green pollen from towering softwoods covered the watery surface like a worn-out overcoat.

It had been a busy few days for Allagash Lake and all the campsites at the north end were full of campers. Doing a quick mental calculation Jim figured that with the four campsites, within easy travel of the camp, there were enough individual cells for 8 parties. And waterway regulations allowed each party to have a maximum of 12 people. *That,* he thought, *means that technically I could be looking at 96 people right this very minute; quite a batch of campers for a place where people work very hard to get away from it all.*

Starting at the Ledge Point site he used the binoculars to scan to the campsites that were within his view. First, he studied the Ledge and Sandy Point sites that were directly across from his cabin where people were just starting to mill around. Gathering in a bunch, in unison, they all were pointing at something out in the lake. Continuing to survey the lake, the ranger turned towards the distant Outlet Campsite where he saw wood smoke hanging over the lake's outlet, *probably some folks who arrived on the lake last night from wading up Allagash Stream. More than likely the campsite at Little Allagash Falls will need cleaning and, more importantly he needed to check to make sure that the campfire had been properly extinguished.*

From where he was standing he couldn't see the Cove Campsite around the point to his right, but he knew there was a party of two people camping there; a man and woman. Proudly declaring they were on their honeymoon when Jim had checked them the previous day, he had examined their permit and then purposely stayed away to respect their privacy. He then swung his gaze to the Ice Cave tent site, the campground closest to and within walking distance to his cabin—only to see the canoes from that site heading out into the lake.

Standing tall the ranger held the eyeglasses with both hands to keep the glasses steady. His 10x50 binoculars quickly showed that some sort of activity was taking place all over the north end of the lake.

Watching paddle blades flash in the sun, the ranger could see that the people from the three campsites had jumped into their canoes and were headed towards the middle of the lake. There the visitors' canoes were sitting unmoving in calm waters and, with their own eyeglasses, were staring towards the two ledge islands that were about a mile to the southeast. Two occupants of the lead canoe seemed to be talking to the others. All of the remaining canoes maneuvered to be in a semi-circle around the speakers. If he didn't know any better he would have guessed that it was a class of students listening to their instructor. Through his field glasses Jim recognized the person doing the talking and smiled quietly to himself, now understanding a part of what was taking place.

Watching for several minutes the ranger started to walk back to his cabin to get his life preserver so he could go out and hear for himself what was going on; when he saw the groups disperse with each canoe heading back to their respective sites. Instead of using his canoe, Jim walked over to the Ice Cave Campsite to greet the nearest party as they came to shore. After the bow of the canoe had scrunched to a landing on the pea gravel beach he said, "It appears to be quite a commotion going on out there."

"Sure was!" the lady in the lead canoe replied.

"Mind if I ask?" said Jim.

"Well it's the funniest thing really. We were enjoying

our morning coffee on the rocks by the shore when we heard a gosh awful noise coming from the lake. There first was a whole bunch of buzzy—'keh-keh' sounds that was soon followed by a harsh 'kee-errr.'

"Then we heard a different clatter. It sounded like a short 'kip' followed by harsh 'tr-tee-ar.' Other people must have heard it as well, because when we jumped into our canoes to check it out, a whole bunch of other campers joined us in the middle of the lake.

"We all looked across the lake where we saw a flotilla of white birds circling the ledge islands to the southeast. While watching, we started speculating about might be happening. Some thought an Eagle had attacked some nesting birds. Others thought a fox had swum out to the island to eat nesting eggs, when a couple in one of the other canoes started sounding real knowledgeable."

Speaking excitedly, the woman climbed out of the bow of the canoe now onto the shore, occasionally turned to look back down the lake and continued talking.

"This guy who began speaking said his name was Bob, introduced his wife Sandi, and said that he could explain what was happening. It seems that there are two species of birds flying around the same island and they are having a quarrel over who can stay there.

"Bob said that the small, slender, white bird making the 'kip' and a harsh 'tr-tee-ar' sound is the Arctic Tern. The tern normally breeds in the Arctic, but for years the little guy with the black cap, nape and white throat and cheek, has been nesting on Allagash Lake; at the southern edge of their typical nesting grounds. The tern will eventually head to its wintering grounds off Antarctica, the farthest yearly journey of any bird. The tern builds its nest on the ground and will return to the area where they were hatched to breed. Terns can live for over 20 years, so most of those birds have been building ground nests on that little island for a very long time.

ARCTIC TERN EGGS ON TERN ISLAND, ALLAGASH LAKE.

(T. CAVERLY PHOTO.)

"Because of the northern nature of Allagash Lake, there is also a bird known as Bonaparte's Gull. The little gull arrives here every year to breed in July or August, and is the only gull to nest in trees.

BONAPARTE'S GULL, ALLAGASH LAKE. (DEAN BENNETT PHOTO.)

"Allagash Lake is beyond its normal nesting range and it is the single lake in the north woods where the birds have been found to nest. Therefore the bird is tied directly to northern Maine's boreal forest.

"It is easy to tell the difference between the gull and tern in that the whole head and bill of the gull is black and it has a square tail, while the tern has a black cap, orange bill, and deeply forked tail. The tail of the tern really stands out because the outer rim of its feathers has highlighted black edges.

"While they have different nesting habits the birds also have different foods. The gull is known to occasionally make shallow plunge dives and feeds chiefly on insects captured from the air or from the surface of lakes and ponds. The neat little guy never eats from man-made dumps. The terns love to eat small fish and crustaceans and make the buzzy 'Keh-keh' sound that we all heard this morning.

"Bob told us more, but I can't remember it all right now. He sure was knowledgeable. Do you know who he might be? Perhaps a doctor, college professor, biologist, or something?"

Smiling the ranger replied, "Yes, I know Bob and his wife very well. They come here quite often and it isn't unusual for them to share their knowledge with others. You've had a special treat today."

"How so?"

"Well the guy you met is Bob Duchesne and for years he was a DJ in radio. In fact, his radio show was so popular that a few years ago he was inducted into the Country DJ Hall of Fame in Nashville. After his radio career he became interested in birds and has become and is one of Maine's top birding experts. He serves on the Audubon Board of Trustees and leads birding trips from Atlantic Canada to the Florida

Everglades. Bob has authored a guidebook for the state and writes a weekly birding column for the *Bangor Daily News*. He is very busy and also has a weekly radio show on 92.9 F.M. called "Wild Maine." As if that wasn't enough, he has also served four terms in Maine's House of Representatives. While in office he served on the Environment and Natural Resources Committee and helped direct our state's environmental policy.

"You've had a real education today and he is always willing to share his expertise and experience."

"Oh yes, I've remembered something else," the woman said. "Bob did say that a group of terns is known as a Ternery or a 'U' and that a flock of Bonaparte's Gulls are known as a flotilla. I asked if the birds nest differently and eat different stuff then why were they squabbling? Bob said they were probably just being protective of their nesting and feeding ground. I am a science teacher and I've learned something today—can't wait to take this all back to my classroom in the fall.

"Oh," she hollered when she saw Jim starting to turn away. "On our way back we also saw the majestic bald eagle sitting on the branch of a tall pine."

Smiling and waving at the woman to show that he had

heard her, Jim walked away. Striding by George, Jim saw that the guy was concentrating on putting something in his day pack. *Wonder what shenanigans the old trickster is up to now?* A growling stomach reminded Jim that he hadn't eaten breakfast yet, so he headed back to the cabin to fry up the trout he had caught the previous night. Taking one last look down at the clouds forming out on the lake he couldn't help but predict *this heat seems to be cooking up a real weather breeder.* Passing the trail sign that pointed the way to the geological formation up the hill, he remembered the article about his grandfather and the strange sounds that people occasionally heard.

Others had told Jim about odd noises heard emanating out of this hole in the earth known as the Ice Cave. However, if he had been told, Jim wouldn't have believed, nor would he have understood—the composition building within the coming storm, nor the intensity of the medley that was being composed in the fissure below.

CHAPTER XXV

Listening intently to everything being said by his neighbors, George grumbled low so the people on the next site couldn't hear—*this ain't the time to be bringing attention to myself.* Watching out of the corner of his good eye, George followed Jim's every movement towards the ranger's camp.

Mumbling, George spoke only to himself, "just don't understand why these darn fools get so excited about a bunch of birds. The whole flock put together ain't worth a wooden nickel. You can't eat 'em, they make poor bait; heck those white feathered things don't even make good garden fertilizer." Working busily George continued to belly ache, "and as for the bald eagle; why that scavenger ain't nothing, but a raven in a tuxedo. Give me a nice feed of partridge or spruce grouse any day for my taste."

Prepared for the day; George sneaked a chainsaw from a nearby fir thicket and concealed it in a large, black, plastic bag. From his cooler he grabbed a Styrofoam container of worms, *just in case I need to catch supper,* and then he slipped a .357 Rugger Speed-Six magnum revolver into his coat pocket. The gun was George's pride and joy. He wouldn't admit to working for money, but he had labored for days to earn enough dough for the handgun. The firearm was the best piece of equipment he ever had. *Besides,* he thought, *you just never knew when an angry moose, deer, or bear might attack. Sure hope it's a deer this time, the last animal that charged sure was ... ,* and here George allowed himself a quiet laugh and finished the private joke with, *tough eatin'.* George smiled to himself at making such a good pun about the illegal moose he'd shot the previous year. Then more serious, he measured, *or maybe we'll just have to take care of some pesky varmint wither it be four legged or two legged.*

If you could have watched the man move around his campsite, you'd never guess that he was over 70 years old. Tall, thin, and still able to walk effortlessly from years of tramping over rough ground; George strolled with the determination of a man with a purpose.

On closer inspection, it was plain that George was a man not to be trifled with. Thin and muscular, always sporting a two-day-old beard, he looked plain mean. It wasn't the beard or callused hands or even the scars that would cause a person to be cautious; as much as the expression on his face.

And then it wasn't even the sharpness of his jaw or the turned-down corners of his razor thin lips, as much as the look of his eyes. And it wasn't both eyes either. The right eye had a clear, deep, intelligent gaze, like it could sight down a rifle barrel and shoot a fly off a bird's beak at 100 yards.

It was the left eye. Useless from an accident years before, the pupil had a ghostly appearance and would glare at a person as if the dead tissue could look directly into a person's heart.

George would never talk about himself, nor would he answer questions if asked; but he'd had a hard existence. George was born late in his mother's life after his father had died in a drowning accident. Being an only child, he didn't have much family. George didn't have any brothers or sisters and he didn't even know the names of either set of grandparents or where they had lived. Although he had heard his mom say once she liked the country and missed trout fishing, she refused to say any more about their past. George might have guessed that they had lived in a more rural area, but couldn't be sure.

Brought up in a large city in southern Maine, George had wandered the streets begging for food and money while his mother worked long hours as a waitress. George loved his mom, but he worried her. Heart broke from losing her husband at a young age, George's mother had hoped her son would be a replica of her late husband, who had been a good, hardworking man, *if he could only be like his dad,* she'd prayed late at night.

But the problem was that the boy didn't have much direction. Polly spent so much time at work trying to make enough money to pay bills, that she was rarely home; leaving George to fend for himself.

Over time the boy fell in with the wrong crowd and in order to be accepted by the group, gave in to pressure to stay up all night drinking hard liquor—although to George's credit, the youngster did stay away from the drugs that were always handy. *Just too expensive to bother with,* he'd thought.

Then one night George got caught on the wrong side of the robbery of a small family-owned business. Trying to fight his way out, George got hit in the left eye, causing permanent loss of sight.

He was sent to reform school and his mother suffered from depression. Blaming herself for the son's misfortune, the woman grieved herself to death (the official cause, as determined by the coroner, was a stroke from very high blood pressure).

After a stint in the reformatory, George was released to a caseworker. The agent saw something in George that others hadn't. She made arrangements for him to have a dishwashing job at a sporting camp deep in the Maine woods—away from the street elements who had claimed to be George's best buds.

At 16, this was George's first attempt at steady work. At first he felt like he had been brought in for grunt labor. When he wasn't washing dishes, he would dig holes for pit privies, cut firewood, and clear blowdowns from hiking trails, as well as dozens of other menial chores. George had told the operators of the camps that he wanted to go back to the city. They asked him to give it another month, and if after 30 days he still wanted to go back, they promised to drive him. George agreed to give life in the woods one more chance.

Then George started noticing things. The smell of the aromatic red pine, the flash from the white tail of a deer startled from a meal of the buds from a wild rose. Then there were the sounds—the White-throated Sparrow that greeted each day with the thin whistle of *Old-Sam-Peabody-Peabody*; the raspy, almost-hoarse call of the Black Duck, and **conk-la-ree** song of the Red-wing Blackbird that happily announced the return of spring.

In the evening he heard the splash of the speckled brook trout feeding on hatches of the May fly. Whenever he fished, George would watch a mother moose taking care of her twin, light brown calves. At night the big dipper was so bright and so close that he could almost reach up and pluck it out of the sky. But it was the loon, that mournful call that resonated through him and touched his soul.

At the end of the 30 days the operators asked George if he still wanted to go back to the city. Slowly shaking his head "no" George explained, "all I hear in the city is the wail of sirens, and I don't want to hear sirens anymore." George had found a home and he quickly became an excellent woodsman. It was about this same time that he decided that drinking whiskey wasn't worth the bother of having a morning headache, and after a brief scolding from a sport about the use of inappropriate language in front of a child; George figured there must be better ways to express his intelligences than by using profanity.

The weeks flew by until one eventful day the forest caught on fire. Rumored to be started by an arsonist, the inferno ultimately burned hundreds of acres. The blaze incinerated everything for miles around; including the sporting camps where George lived. Everything the adolescent owned, including his brand new Fenwick fly rod, was lost.

Nobody knew how the fire started; some suspected it was an arsonist's attempt to punish the landowner for closing roads. Others said it was a person needing a job so he set the woodlands on fire to get work. A third even suggested that someone had lit a match just to see stuff burn. Whatever the reason, it was George who got blamed. The sporting camp owners told George that they didn't suspect him, but they had lost everything they owned and the business didn't have insurance. So there wasn't a place for him to stay, much less work.

Time would prove that the blaze had been caused by lightning, but the accusations left a nasty taste in George's mouth. He was spurned by the forest community—in return

George rejected them. That is when he turned really sour and figured; *if people feel I am no good—then why disappointment 'em.*

Then George heard about Allagash Lake and the fish that were so plentiful you could scoop them up in your hands. The first time he ever canoed down the stream and into the lake, George thought *now this is the way to get to somewhere, by canoe.* Entering the large lake a nearby loon offered its welcoming tremolo call. George felt like he'd come home.

It was early spring during in Dalton's fourth summer working on Allagash Lake when he caught George fishing illegally at the lake's inlet. Noticing a bobber floating in the water Dalton had summons George for fishing with worms in an area where the law allowed only the use of artificial lures. This was George's first appearance before a judge since he had been in juvenile court years before.

That started a battle between the ranger and the poacher. George would do things to aggravate Dalton whenever possible.

He would play such tricks as hiding short trout in the woodpile at the ranger's camp or look for ways to drive his vehicle to the shore of the lake. Now George knew that this was a designated wilderness area and the use of a pickup within one mile of the lake was prohibited; so he loved to leave tire marks right down to the water. He'd cut the legs from the carcass of a moose killed by disease and leave them on Dalton's porch so the ranger would think the animal had been poached. And there were dozens of other tricks.

As far as Dalton was concerned, he had very little regard for George and would go out of his way to watch for his nemesis and wait for him to make a mistake. The two never carried on a pleasant conversation, nor helped the other, and that is the way they both liked it.

CHAPTER XXVI

Waking before dawn, as had become his habit, Jim dressed and walked down to the dock to check the morning's weather. He was surprised to see that George was already in his canoe and heading off, once again, towards the east and the stream.

There goes the old guy again. Awful early, wonder if he's using worms to fish the pool below Otter Stream or at the falls? Guess I'd better find out.

Not one to waste the coming daylight, Jim prepared his equipment expecting to be on the water for a whole day. An hour later the ranger pulled up to the landing at the Outlet, near the spot where the lake flowed into the lower stream. From his canoe, Jim could see the wooden remains of a wing from an old roll dam. This recollection from the days of spring river drives, spoke volumes about a period long forgotten.

Walking across the campsite and down a fisherman's trail on the north side of the stream, Jim checked for any sign of George's canoe. Not finding any he returned to his canoe and using the portable two-way radio he contacted Warden Farrar by using the warden's call sign,

"1703 to 2248."

"10-3[go ahead], 1703."

"Are you going to be anywhere near Little Allagash Falls today? I believe our friend may be fishing illegally."

10-4, 1703, I am near there now and will check it out."

"10-4."

"Thanks for the information. 2248 clear."

Within minutes Jim received a second call from the watchperson that lived at the south end of the lake.

"Allagash Mountain to 1703."

"10-3 Allagash Mountain."

"We have a medical emergency, are you available to assist?"

"10-4. What is the nature of the emergency?"

"We have a scout troop at the Carry Trail site and a counselor has reported that one of the young scouts has cut herself with an axe. Another leader has started triage."

"I copied and I am on the way."

Starting his outboard and heading down the lake, Jim continued with his radio traffic and called the Department of Conservation's dispatcher; "1703 to Ashland."

"10-3, 1703."

"Alert tour aircraft that we have a medical emergency on Allagash Lake and we may need a transport to the hospital."

"10-4, 1703. The pilot has been alerted."

Approaching the campsite at the south end of the lake, Jim could see a group of girls gathered in a circle. Running his canoe onto the gravel beach, he shut off the outboard, grabbed his first aid kit, and jumped onto shore. Quickly pulling the bow onto dry land, he hurried towards the group.

Seeing the ranger arrive, the circle of scouts parted to expose a girl lying on a sleeping bag spread out over the ground. Kneeling over the teenager, a black-haired lady was applying pressure to the girl's right leg. A bloody bandage already soaked dark red was evidence that the young scout had received a very bad cut.

Kneeling next to the leader, Jim asked, "How can I help?" The counselor raised her head to answer and Jim looked into the deepest hazel green eyes that he remembered so well, and the gaze of Susan.

Returning Jim's stare, Susan said, "this morning she was using an axe and it slipped—she may have nicked an artery; it's a very deep wound. I've applied pressure to the cut but she needs to go to a hospital."

Without replying Jim picked up the microphone of his radio and called, "1703 to Ashland."

Immediately the dispatcher replied, "10-3."

"I am at the scene, please dispatch the floatplane to the Carry Trail Campsite on Allagash Lake. We have a 13-year-old girl who has a severe wound to the artery of her right leg. Pressure has been applied to the wound, and a tourniquet is in place. The girl is stable for now, but she needs to go to the hospital."

"The plane has taken off and will be there shortly, and we'll have an ambulance waiting."

"Thank you, Ashland."

Within minutes Jim received a radio call from the state aircraft;

"930 to 1703."

"Go ahead 930."

"I'll be there in 5 minutes, is the landing site secure?

"10-4, 930. Come on in."

Then the group heard the welcome hum of a floatplane

circling overhead. Once the pilot had identified where to land, he sat down on the water and taxied into shore. Jim ran to the seaplane, grabbed a stretcher from the back seat, and carried it to the girl. While Susan maintained pressure on the wound, Jim, the pilot, and another leader settled the girl into the litter and placed her on the floor of the aircraft.

Climbing on board to accompany her scout, Susan turned to Jim and said, "I need to go with her to the hospital." Looking intently at Jim, she said, "I got your phone message, and I do to."

Susan then smiled and blushed with, "I'll be back as soon as I can."

With that the plane took off to meet the waiting EMTs.

Jim checked with the other leaders to make sure the scene was safe, took statements for the official report, and then headed back into the canoe and out onto the lake. Motoring by the Ede's Campsite Jim received a radio message from Warden Farrar.

"2248 to 1703."

"10-3, 2248."

"I am at the falls and there isn't any sign of our suspect."

"10-4, I copied" Jim replied.

"I spoke with a group of four headed upstream. It is the Warren Cochrane party and they should be at the Outlet Campsite by nightfall. "

"10-4, 2248. Thanks, Bruce."

"10-4. Glad to help."

Jim was happy to hear that the Cochranes were on the way. Warren was the second generation owner and operator of the respected Allagash Canoe Trips guide service. With his partner Linda, son Chip, and daughter-in-law Lani; the Cochranes have been conducting quality trips down the Allagash for over 60 years. Jim had heard that the Master Maine Guides had always taken very good care of their sports; and the legendary family had canoed the river so much that Jim always learned something new whenever they spoke.

*****

Noticing two 20-foot, green canvas-covered canoes upside down on the beach by the Outlet Campsite, Jim pulled up to check camping permits. As he landed, a rugged blond man walked down to extend a welcome and help the ranger land his craft, a smiling Warren offered "We've got coffee on, do you have time to stop?"

"Only for a minute, how's the water in the stream?"

"It's a little low," the guide replied. But we were able to pole most of it." And then the tanned man asked, "Is Seven Islands cutting wood to the north of here?"

"Don't think so, why?" inquired the ranger.

"Well coming up the stream, we kept hearing a chainsaw cutting wood. Never did hear any other equipment such as a skidder or truck though, and the sound wasn't continuous. First the power saw would run for a while and then it would stop. Then it would begin again and then quit. Then the sound would go again for a while again. Didn't sound like a normal harvest operation to me."

"How far away would you say it was?"

"Oh downstream about a quarter of a mile or so; and oh yes, there was a canoe pulled into the woods on the north side of the stream. It looked like someone was trying to conceal it, but it wasn't far enough from the water to be completely hidden. Whose ever it is, the person did a poor job of hiding it."

"Would it have been a Grumman with a black outboard motor hung off the left side?"

"Come to think of it, it was an aluminum canoe, looked a lot like yours. I thought it was kind of odd to see a metal canoe there—you know how bad they stick to rocks. Do you know whose it might be?"

"I've got an idea, guess I'll walk down to check."

"Oh it's too late now. That canoe has already come up stream and gone back out to the lake." Warren pointed up the lake and said, "He was headed along the sand beach, by the north shore."

Needing to investigate further, Jim said, "Ok. I'll take a walk anyway to see what I can find. I'll be back in a few minutes."

"Holler if you need help," offered Warren.

Leaving his canoe on shore, Jim walked down the fisherman's trail along the north side of the stream. Passing by the tributary of Otter Pond that joined the stream from the south, he soon entered a stand of mixed hardwoods. Watching for any sign of activity Jim scanned the ground and the forest around him.

Soon he came across a path that led perpendicular from the stream up onto a small hardwood ridge. The trail was well worn and looked like something a very busy beaver would have made. Following the track Jim soon discovered a small cabin.

"Well I'll be darn, so this is what the goober has been up to, thought Jim. *He's built a trapper's line camp right here along the Waterway.* Watching for any signs of an entrapment, Jim walked around the rustic structure.

19TH-CENTURY TRAPPER'S LINE CAMP.

PHOTOGRAPH COURTESY OF THE MAINE FOREST AND LOGGING MUSEUM,

BRADLEY, MAINE.

Placed so as not to be seen by anyone traveling on the stream, the camp had been fabricated from nearby materials. Solidly built out of standing rounded logs nailed side by side, the small house measured 8 feet x 10 feet and was big enough for one person and their gear. The sills had been built on six large flat stones placed equal distant around the camp to keep the foundation off the ground.

On the southeast side of the building was a 24-inch-wide x 66-inch-tall door. This location ensured that an open entrance could capture any warmth offered by a morning sun. The exterior panels of the door were covered with sheets of birch bark so that somebody using a flashlight at night could easily pick up the brightness of the entrance. Hinges for the door were nothing more than cutout pieces of leather straps. The doorknob was one stick horizontally nailed midway up the door, that when closed, would ride up over another that stuck out perpendicular from the frame. By sliding one stick over the other, entrance to the building could be gained, or by pulling a small rope on the inside, the door could be closed.

Windows on the east and west side of the building offered light to the inside. The roof had pole trusses and was sealed from the weather by cedar shakes. A six-inch, metal stovepipe stuck through the north side of the roof proved there would be an opportunity to have a warming fire inside. A long and narrow cabinet nailed along the exterior of the east walls offered a chance to store cold supplies or, more importantly, trapping scent outside.

Entering the building, Jim saw that the interior was designed for convenience and to utilize all available space. The floor was built of split logs with the flat side up. Along the north wall Jim saw a cutout in the floor that measured about 2½ feet x 3½ feet. The hole, partially filled with sand, was waiting for a woodstove to be delivered. Along one wall there was a sturdy bunk laced with fresh balsam fir boughs. The bed, high enough to store pack baskets, lots of wood and canned goods under, was wide enough to sleep one person comfortably on the fragrant mattress.

On the opposite wall, underneath the window, sat an iron sink. The basin had been set into a narrow shelf that ran the length of the wall. It was a ledge which could serve a dual purpose of either a biscuit board or an eating table.

Situated throughout the camp, in strategic places, were

an assortment of forked branches cut to serve as coat hooks and as places to dry wet gear. Along the wall near the door there hung a variety of traps waiting for the coming fur season.

Between the rafters, the carpenter had inlaid large squares of the white side of birch bark, so any light from a candle or kerosene lamp could be reflected back into the interior.

Nice job, George, thought Jim. *I wouldn't mind having a camp like this myself. The workmanship exhibited here is certainly a different picture than George presents to open view. I wonder if there is more to the old guy than meets the eye?* Closing the door Jim spoke out loud saying, "guess I better go have a little talk with our friend."

Walking back along the trail to his canoe Jim noticed several game trails in the area and then he realized the camp was only about ½ mile from a logging road.

Hum, the old timer put a lot of thought in this project. Boy, Dalton would like to have seen this. At the cobblestone beach by the tent site, and without any words, Jim waved to Warren and Linda and climbed back into his canoe. Motoring up the lake, Jim watched for any sign of his nemesis, but

George wasn't anywhere to be seen.

Cruising slowly up the lake Jim couldn't help but ponder where in the world can George be now?

Wonder how the Girl Scout from this morning is doing? And then the earlier conversation finally sunk in, Susan will be coming back and she misses me too!

Little did Jim know that before the evening was over, he'd have bigger things on his mind than George, the cabin, or even Susan.

CHAPTER XXVII

By the time Jim returned to camp and tied his canoe to the dock, the sun had gone down and the moon had come up, lighting the path to the man's home. Dragging feet that weighed a ton, Jim remembered that when he had left that morning, the trail from his cabin was like walking down a gentle slope. Returning now at the end of a long day, the man felt like he was climbing a mountain.

Too tired to cook supper, he lit the gas light, opened the refrigerator, and grabbed the leftover ham from the previous night's supper. Famished, he placed a thick slab of meat between two pieces of bread without even bothering with mustard. Washing down the cold meal with a glass of milk; Jim subconsciously picked up the 1927 copy of "In the Maine Woods" sitting on the table. Jim opened the page to the piece about the Ice Caves and studied the picture of three men who had claimed the photograph was taken 75 feet underground.

Then he heard it. A loud buzzing sound that reminded him of an irritable static drone that pours out of worn-out speakers of a radio experiencing bad reception. And the hum, a deafening hubbub, built in intensity and came from the direction of the Ice Caves. Walking to the door of his camp, Jim thought, *what in the world can that old codger be up to now? This has been a very long, day—I really don't need to deal with him tonight.*

Sighing, he grabbed his flashlight and followed the beam of his Maglite down an auxiliary trail, over a wooden plank, and across a small stream east of camp. This makeshift bridge highlighted a small path that directed him towards the sound. Entering the compacted ground of the campsite, Jim walked by George's tent and noticed that his adversary wasn't there and worse yet, neither was his canoe. *And it's too dark for him to be traveling on the water,* Jim observed.

And then he discovered the cause of the buzzing—lightning bugs.

*****

It wasn't just a few bugs either—but a mass of fireflies that came in low over the water from the east like a squadron of jet fighters, and hummed directly to the trail leading to the Ice Caves. Reaching their destination, the insects touched down one after another, in a perfect line, creating two distinct edges along the path. Jim stood in awe as he watched the glow from the bellies of the little beetles illuminate, like a rows of LED lights, the trail up the hill to the entrance of the cavern.

Walking between the glowing lines, Jim followed the fairylike lights up the trail all the way to the opening of the cave. There the flickering beams continued underground. Stepping off the first rock step at the entrance to the underground, Jim couldn't help but notice that it resembled a giant mouth ready to swallow him whole. Ready to turn around, Jim saw a coin hanging from a ribbon swinging lightly in the night air. The currency, a large copper penny, was suspended at the end of a blue cloth loop and dangled from the end of an exposed tree root. Remembering his grandfather's story, Jim slipped the tie around his neck. The buzzing quieted. The lower volume of noise allowed Jim to hear voices coming from down in the ground. Walking downward into the opening, he arrived at the first cavern. There he saw a slightly out-of-focus picture flickering across a smooth portion of the stone wall. The radiance from the lightning bugs stopped here.

It was a scene of two people in a birch bark canoe; each passenger wore leather shirts, girdled at the waist by a wide leather belt, and tucked into the sash were tools. Each one had a stone knife hanging, suspended off the left side of their belt, while a tomahawk dangled in the same strap, near their right hand.

In the front of the canoe Jim could see a bow with arrows, waiting for a moose to appear. They were paddling out of the outlet, then they stopped near the ledges. There the two men threw a net into the water and immediately brought in a harvest of fish.

That view faded and a new vista appeared. It was an outlook to the south where a huge plume of smoke hovered over far away Mt. Katahdin. The image flickered and a new illustration appeared. The scene was of a man in a single canoe. He was paddling onto the lake, towards the tenting ground at the Ice Caves. His face was soot covered, like he'd had been battling a hot blaze. He was wearing a ribbon around his neck. The man in the canoe looked so much like Jim, they could have been twins.

Now the trail of fireflies once again lit up and led Jim down to a second cavern. There a new graphic panned across the wet rock. It is of a canvas shelter called a baker's tent. The shelter with a high front, resembling the same shape as a reflector oven, sits on the cobblestone shore near the place where the water leaves the lake. There are five men sitting around a campfire, eating. The date 1919 passes across the bottom of the view, and one of the men says, "Tomorrow we should reach the T8R15 town line so we can begin cruising for timber and establish the boundary line."

The picture fast forwarded to the cove in front of Sandy Point. There is a series of log booms leading from the ledge island east of Sandy Point across to the nearest point of land to the south. On the island the boom is anchored to a large iron ring by a 3-inch-wide links of a chain. On the shore to the south, the other end of the log container is anchored by a 1¼-inch steel cable wrapped around the base of a large white pine.

The cove behind the boom is filling with pulp wood and there is more timber floating in by the minute. Men are in bateaus sorting the floating logs when one lumberjack falls overboard. Others reach for him, but the cutter disappears below the surface.

Glowing intensely once again, the illumination of lightning bugs directs Jim even farther underground to a third underground cavity, once there the light from the fireflies dim. A new image is one of bright colors of autumn foliage. The hardwood leafs are bright reds, yellows, and gold—it is fall. There is a man in uniform standing on a sandy beach. Behind him is a white sign indicating that he is near a designated campsite. The man's boat has drifted away. It is the forest warden's only mode of transportation. He removes his clothes, folds them, and places them on a nearby log. He begins swimming, but sinks in the cold water and doesn't resurface. Here the trail of fireflies once again light up, leading Jim farther down and into a fourth compartment. The opening is narrow and Jim is barely able to squeeze through. But he forces his way in and once again a movie flickers on the smooth rocky wall before him.

It's almost dark and there is a canoe motoring across the lake, coming from the direction of the Outlet. The face of the person in the canoe is obscured. But the man has the same build as Jim, but he isn't wearing a lifejacket. Suddenly a gust of wind comes up and overturns the canoe. An anchor, tied to the bow by rope, falls out and holds the boat in place; in the middle of the lake. The man is in the water. He is trying to holler, Jim can't hear what the man is saying. The boatman is holding onto the crossbar of the canoe. He grabs a piece of cord floating nearby and ties his left hand to the thwart. A caption floats across the bottom of the screen with only one word—**CLARK**.

Could this be a prediction of my death? Jim couldn't help but speculate about his own demise.

Then another image appears. Strangely out of place, it shows two people standing at an altar. The woman is wearing a wedding gown, and in the image; the woman turns and looks at something behind her. Jim recognizes it is Susan, but can't tell who the man is. The fellow is wearing a gray suit and a golden retriever puppy sits by his side. The dog is patiently holding a white basket with a ring in it, and then the picture recedes.

The fireflies extinguish their glow in front of Jim, and as he turns to snap on his flashlight, he notices that the lightning bugs are now glowing behind him, back up the trail. Another image flashes onto the rock wall near the entrance. It is of his dad hiking up the trail to the Caves. His father is carrying the same coin and ribbon that Jim is wearing. After he hangs it off the tree root at the entrance to the cave the picture extinguishes like a match that has been blown out. Once again the path is lit by little dots of yellow leading the way out.

CAVE OF FIREFLIES

CHAPTER XXVIII

Jim awoke face down, with his arms sprawled across a copy of the travel log that he'd been reading just a few hours before. Its dawn and he is still sitting at the kitchen table, where he had eaten supper and collapsed into a deep sleep.

Last night! Could that have possible happened? Still feeling exhausted, Jim shakes the sleep cobwebs out of his head and remembers the visions still so very vivid in his mind. Imagining and hoping the vision is only a delusion he thinks, *that could not have possibly happened. Must have been just a dream!*

Convinced that the vision had been only a fantasy, Jim remembered that he needed to find George, and so he arose from the table where he'd been sitting. When he stood up, Jim felt something swing against his neck. Looking down, he saw an 1838 copper penny with the initials JPC stamped on the coin's obverse hanging off a frayed ribbon. It was the coin in his dream. *Well I'll be darned–guess this part is; well ... real.*

Slowly coming to his senses, he walked out the door of the camp, toward his canoe. Grabbing his binoculars and his emergency day pack along the way, he stood on the dock and, using his field glasses, he surveyed the lake. Scanning the north shore, he quickly picked up the glint of something long and silver, holding steady about a mile down the lake roughly 300 yards from the beach.

Remembering the prophecy from last night, Jim slipped on a life jacket and hurriedly jumped into his canoe. Yanking the outboard motor's rewind cord, the engine came to life with the first pull. Underway, the ranger cruised at wide open speed splitting the budding white caps cresting across the lake's surface.

Arriving at the shiny object, Jim found George's canoe lying on its side and bobbing like a giant apple in the waves of a northwest wind. The Mercury outboard, still hooked to the mount on the side of the canoe, was lying horizontal in the water. A red gas tank floating nearby was held to the craft by a black umbilical gas line.

The canoe had a rope tied off at the bow that led straight down towards the deep recess of the lake. Jim quickly realized that an anchor had fallen out of the watercraft and it now served as a mooring, secure the canoe in place. In the distance, a wooden paddle floated away with the waves.

Getting closer to the overturned canoe, he could see a hand peaking over the edge, desperately tied by a nylon cord to the canoe's thwart. There wasn't a life jacket in sight.

Moving to the other side of the 20-foot craft, Jim saw that George was hanging on by a thread. His face was turned sideways partially out of water but the color of his face was an ash white. George's bad eye stared, unseeing, straight up in the air.

Shifting his motor into neutral, Jim knelt on the bottom of his canoe to keep his center of gravity low. Once positioned, he used his belt knife to free the man tied to the swamped canoe. George's body remained on the surface for a second, lurched and began to sink. With one hand the rescuer grabbed the victim by his collar and with his other, slipped it under the back of George's belt. Careful not to tilt his own canoe too far, Jim rolled the unconscious man into the rescue canoe. A brisk wind bounced the ranger's canoe from side to side. Once George was on the floor of his canoe, Jim bent down and placed two fingers on the side of George's neck. Jim felt a slight pulse. Thank goodness, Jim thought the man isn't dead.

Once in the canoe, George coughed, but his good eye remained closed—unseeing. His canoe is anchored in place and won't be going anywhere, Jim said to himself as he shifted his own motor into gear and headed back towards camp. When he passed the Ice Cave Campsite, he noticed the same troop of scouts from the previous day had paddled up the land and were watching him from the shore. Seeing Susan on shore, he slowed and hollered, "Susan, can you help? I've got someone here who is near death. There is a trail to my camp right behind that green tent. We might be able to save him." The leader waved that she understood, turned to give instructions to the other leaders, and headed through the woods.

By the time Jim had pulled up to the wharf, Susan was already there and she held the canoe while Jim rolled the unconscious body out onto the wooden dock pitching with the waves. Carrying George like a rag doll, Jim lugged George on his back into camp. Instructing Susan to build a fire and heat water, Jim took George into the spare bedroom, stripped him down to his shorts and with a towel rubbed the cold, wet man dry. *At least he is still alive,* Jim thought feeling very relieved to see the man's chest slowly rise and fall with a labored breath.

Placing George in bed and covering him with warm blankets, Susan held the unconscious man's head up and dabbed warm tea onto blue lips. The man's tongue unconsciously licked his mouth and he swallowed. George then groaned and inhaled softly. Seeing that the victim was able to accept liquid, Susan offered him a teaspoon of tea.

After George had swallowed the liquid, she laid George's head softly down onto a pillow and tucked blankets in around him, and left him to rest. Susan turned to Jim and said, "guess, I, ahh, should be really, well, be getting back to my, ahhh, troop now, to help set up camp."

Hopefully Jim invited, "can you stay for a bit to watch George? I'd like to visit. But I need to take care of that overturned canoe first." Susan looked anxiously at Jim so he explained, "If I don't go back, then someone from one of the campsites might try and pull it to shore. And if they attempt to do so in this rough water, I am apt to have another rescue on my hands."

Susan nodded that she understood and Jim left.

By the time he returned with all of George's equipment, Susan had made a fresh pot of coffee. Shivering from being soaking wet himself, Jim took a welcome sip of the hot liquid, changed his clothes, and then he and Susan talked. Catching up on the years since Jim had left school, the man and woman talked, and talked, and then talked some more. Jim explained what had happened to him since college, and Susan chatted about graduating from the university and that she was now teaching science in the Millinocket Middle School.

Hearing George stir from the other room, Jim invited, "I've got some days off coming up and I need to go to town for supplies. If you don't mind I'd like to take you to dinner when I get to Millinocket."

Susan smiled and said, "I'd like that."

And then Jim heard a shout coming from the bedroom demanding, "Hey! Who stole my clothes?"

*****

Smiling Susan rose from the table and said, "Guess I'll be getting back to my girls now."

Walking her to the porch door, Jim promised to call and listened to Susan hum softly as she dreamily walked down the trail.

Shuffling out of the bedroom, George appeared in the

doorway wrapped in a blanket. Jim gave him a spare set of clothes and poured him a cup of coffee.

Sitting at the table, George felt humbled by needing to be rescued so he freely explained what had happened. When he had left the outlet the previous day that the wind had been coming heavy out of the northwest. *Yes, he had seen Jim go by, but he had hid on shore until the ranger was out of sight.* With the wind blowing away from the ranger's camp, George had thought he could use his outboard motor to sneak across the lake and back to his campsite. But an unexpected gust from the southeast had caught the man in a cross current and before George knew it he was in the water.

When the canoe tipped over the anchor had fallen out of the bow, mooring the canoe in the middle of the lake. The hunting knife he kept on his belt had fallen out and he couldn't untie the anchor rope. George had tried hollering for help, but no one could hear his shouts over the gusty roar of the wind. Afraid he was going to drown George then tied his left hand to the crossbar of the canoe, and spent the night trying to keep his head above water, until he finally lost consciousness. George had remained that way all night.

Thankful to be alive, George stated "well, this has been a pod-auger day"* and then thanked Jim again for saving his life. The man then admitted that he had set up camp at the Ice Caves so he could keep an eye on the ranger. George, red faced, confessed to building the camp, and yes he knew it was illegal to do so; and if Jim wouldn't arrest him, he promised to tear the camp down, and haul it all away.

George then added "you probably know Jim that Dalton and I don't get along. Well I am tired of arguing, and my promise to you is that I'll never pull any tricks on anyone again. Allagash Lake means a lot to me. But if you want me to leave and never come back, I will do so. It's the least I can do to repay what you did."

"No George, you don't need to do that. I'll take you at your word. But," and here Jim emphasized, "I'll only trust you this once. Let me down and we'll seek a legal injunction prohibiting you from ever being on the lake again."

---

* Pod-auger day: a pod-auger was a type of large drill used to make wooden water pipes. A pod-auger day is an old woodsman's term meaning "it's been a long, hard day."

Then to soften his words, Jim offered, "by the way I am going out for days off and you'd do me a favor if I can sign you on as a volunteer, and ask you to watch the lake while I'm gone."

Staring at the ranger with open mouth, George stuck his hand out to shake hands and replied with a huge smile, "I'd be honored and rest assured I won't do anything to make you sorry you trusted me." George looked Jim in the eye, smiled and thought, *it's been a long time since anyone had put such faith in me. I'm not gonna fail him.*

"By the way, George, I don't know your last name. I need it for the volunteer form."

"It's Clark. My full name is George Paul Clark. My grandma was married to an old-timer known as Jim Paul Clark. My mom was named for her and called Polly, her real name was Pauline.

CHAPTER XXIX

It's Friday afternoon and Jim is heading up Allagash Stream to reach a Waterway 4x4 that has been left at the put-in for him to use. Hearing a noise coming his way, he shuts off his outboard motor and meets a canoe that is loaded with enough camping equipment for a stay of several days. A pretty lady sits in the bow; a young girl is seated in a canoe seat in the middle, and in the stern sits a man with a golden retriever resting comfortably between his bent knees.

"You folks headed to the lake?" Jim inquires.

"Yes," the woman in the front of the canoe answers. "We hope to camp at Sandy Point. I used to stay there with my dad and mom. Do you know if the site is open?"

"Yes, you're in luck. There is only one person on the lake, and he is filling in for me at the ranger's camp. Do you know where that building is?"

"Oh, yes," the lady replied with a wide smile that indicated she knew a secret.

Wanting to get into the conversation the little girl excitedly blurted, "My Pépé used to work here and this is my first trip to the lake."

Then the dog stood and wagged its tail at Jim as if it needed to say hello as well. So the man ordered, "Sit still, Allie." And with that command ending the conversation, Jim waved, offered an "enjoy your visit," and started his outboard to continue up stream.

*****

Later that day Jim reached Millinocket to begin his days off. He picked up his personal car, did a load of laundry, stopped at the hardware store and bought a few assorted tools for the camp. Seeing Ferland's Jewelry shop on the town's main street, Jim decided to stop and make a purchase. Then it was off to the post office to get his mail and then pick up Susan for dinner. Opening his post office box, he found an official looking letter sitting on top of the three-week long pile of correspondence. He noticed that it carries the return address of the Waterway Supervisor, Leigh Smith.

Worried that it might be bad news, Jim immediately opened the dispatch and read;

Maine Department of Conservation
Bureau of Parks and Lands
Allagash Wilderness Waterway
P.O. Box 365
Millinocket, Maine 04462

Mr. James Clark
General Delivery

Millinocket, Maine 04462

Dear Jim,

The ranger, who has been working at Allagash Lake for the last several years, has decided to resign from that position. Therefore, the Department will be accepting applications and conducting interviews to offer seasonal employment to the most qualified candidate.

You are invited to complete the enclosed application and you have been scheduled to appear before the interview board at my office on Katahdin Avenue next Monday at 9 A.M. Please bring the completed application with you to the interview.

Sincerely,

Leigh

Leigh Smith, Superintendent

Smiling, he read the letter again and then jumped into the blue Comet to get Susan for their arranged dinner at the Scootic In Restaurant. Beside him on the passenger's seat, encased in a velvet-covered jewelry box, a diamond engagement ring glittered and awaited its moment.

Driving off towards Penobscot Avenue, Jim rubbed the coin still hanging around his neck and thought, *Hope my luck holds!*

EPILOGUE

In the Forest

I went for a walk

And what did I see?

Why all kinds of things

That surrounded me.

There were trees and flowers and wildlife and such.

I even found trains, and Indian things;

I never dreamed

there could be so much!

Jim Clark

Allagash Lake

Two years later at a community burial ground in central Maine ...

A tall stranger stops at the entrance of a cemetery and scans the oceans of gravestones laid out in neat rows. The man's skin is tanned deep brown and he walks straight and proud from his work in the forests of Maine. Passing through the wrought iron gate he sees marble statues sitting majestically on green manicured plots; paying tribute to those interred, men and women who had once walked the earth.

The man had come to pay his respects to someone he's never met—a grandfather— his Pépé—a man who died before he was born. A visitor to this hallowed ground, the man had been surprised several years before when he discovered a letter from this deceased relative. This message from the past was his only connection with a grandfather he'd only heard about.

Entering the sanctuary the caller examines the monuments for any sign of his family name. After a few minutes of searching he finds a gravestone that proudly displays the household name of Clark. Locating his grandfather's memorial he bends down and with gentle hands brushes away the green moss that has begun to fill in the chiseled letters and reads ...

JAMES PAUL CLARK

BORN NOVEMBER 16, 1938

DIED JUNE 1, 1993

THE SPIRIT STILL LINGERS IN A FOREST PLACE ....

Caressing the carved lettering of his grandpa's name, the man felt the tingle of a slight electrical shock prickle through his body. Touching the cold headstone, the woodsman reflects about what he knew about this man he's never met.

As a child the stranger had learned how his grandfather loved to hunt and fish and as a young boy had explored Maine from Sebago Lake to Baxter Park. Although his grandfather had loved the woods, his grandpa's time had been consumed with raising a family and running a business. Even so there were those who said that he'd been a rugged man who had a keen sense of humor and sometimes liked to write poetry. The grandson had also been told that he was the spitting image, in look and mannerisms of his Pépé.

Deep in thought, the tall man remained quiet for several minutes and finally spoke to this representation of a man who seemed larger than life and said, "Hi Gramps, we've never met, but my name is Jim and I read your letter."

Jim then removed a narrow ribbon from around his neck.

Hanging off the end of the necklace dangled a large 1838 Liberty penny. For a moment the visitor studied the slightly tarnished surface of the antique coin that still captured the reflection of the sun. Jim briefly pondered the good luck the currency represented, and then carefully draped the medallion so it hung like a medal over the stone. With his mission accomplished, Jim straightened and turned to walk to his vehicle. As he moved away the coin invisibly melted into the monument perhaps in preparation for another assignment.

Back in the parking lot the bronzed man opened the driver's door of the crew cab and woke a golden retriever sleeping on the back seat. Katahdin's Allagash Sandy Point immediately picked up her head and wagged her tail to welcome the master's return. Scratching the dog's ear the gentleman said to his pet, "Well Sandy, what do you say we head back to the woods? We'll pick up the wife, Jim Jr., and little George en route. Gramps would have wanted it that way."

And with that Allagash Ranger James Paul Clark drove home....

THE END

(OR IS IT?)

AFTERWARD

"There is a place; where snow blankets a frozen forest and the only sound heard is the snapping of ice-covered softwoods—shivering in protest under the cold glow of the northern lights.

Maine Department of Conservation
Bureau of Parks and Lands
Allagash Wilderness Waterway
P.O. Box 365
Millinocket, Maine 04462

Mr. James Clark, Allagash Ranger
P.O. Box 626
Clayton Lake, Maine 04737

Dear Jim,

I am writing to express my appreciation for your work in the Allagash Lake District over these past years. Your attention to detail and extreme resourcefulness when faced with unknown situations that need immediate attention is recognized and appreciated.

Because of your obligation to duty, I am pleased to offer you a year-round position, where during the winter you'll live at Churchill Dam. As we discussed last week, you are assigned to move into the ranger's camp by Nov. 14, 2016 and work from there until May 1, 2017; when you are scheduled to report back to the Allagash Lake District.

Your duties will include assignments all along the 92 mile length of the Waterway and you will discover that the cold weather operations are quite demanding. I am confident that you have the personal resources, resilience, and stamina necessary to fulfill your duties while working in extreme arctic conditions.

Sincerely,
Leigh
Leigh Smith, Superintendent

THIS BOOK HAS RECEIVED THE MISTY DOG "NOSE TOUCH OF APPROVAL."

KATAHDIN'S ALLAGASH MIST AKA MISTY. (T. CAVERLY PHOTO.)

After examining the book Misty critiqued;

"I was held captive by the story Streaming. I couldn't wait to turn to the next page. I laughed, I cried, and at one point I got so excited I barked. This story is so good I think even Jasmine the cat would enjoy it"

ABOUT THE AUTHOR:
TIM CAVERLY

TIM AS A YOUNG HIKER, AT RUSSELL POND, BSP CIRCA 1962.
(NOTE: THE PIPE IS A PICTURE PROP, IT DIDN'T CONTAIN TOBACCO.)

T. CAVERLY PHOTO

Tim is a Maine author who worked for the Department of Conservation for thirty-two years. During that career he was the manager of Aroostook and Cobscook Bay State Parks and spent eighteen years as Regional Supervisor of the Allagash Region. In 1999, Tim retired from state service and began a second career in the Millinocket school system, where he worked for five years.

Tim currently lives in Millinocket with his wife, Susan and Sandy, their golden retriever. Tim has written six books about the north woods, one of which, An Allagash Haunting, has been made into a stage play and adapted into an "over the air" radio broadcast.

Tim and Susan have been invited to speak about their books and experiences at countless schools, libraries, retirement communities, and colleges throughout New England. And through their "New England Reads" program the couple encourages others to read and explore our spectacular natural world.

ABOUT THE ILLUSTRATOR: FRANKLIN MANZO JR.

FRANK WITH "THE BOYS" IN HIS HOME STUDIO.
(PHOTO BY FSM PHOTOGRAPHY)

Frank was born and raised in Millinocket, Maine where he attended Stearns High School. He retired to his family homestead after working as a software engineer for over 25 years. He has since worked as the Editor of a local newspaper, is noted as a local photographer, and also works in the Millinocket School System.

Frank has always enjoyed pursuing art and sharing his drawings with his children. He is an avid hiker and enjoys being able to share his love of the North Maine Woods by illustrating these Allagash Tails.

Be sure to check out our full line of products from the
ALLAGASH TAILS COLLECTION

Other books by Tim Caverly and Franklin Manzo:
ALLAGASH TAILS VOLUME I

Swim with Marvin Merganser, a fish-eating duck that usually has very bad luck, but his sympathy for a watery neighbor changes all of that. Feel compassion for Charlie the White Water Beaver. Charlie is cross-eyed and narrow tailed who dreams of a better life. See if he can overcome life's adversities in this charming "tail" for the ages.

ALLAGASH TAILS VOLUME II
An Allagash Haunting—The Story of Emile Camile

A damping cloak of darkness approaches . . ." A violent Thunder storm is building and ten-year-old Olivia is canoeing and camping deep in the Maine woods.

Travel with the little girl as she learns about one of our nation's wild rivers and discovers an unknown secret about her mother; when she comes face to face with the last thing anyone could expect.

ALLAGASH TAILS VOLUME III

Wilderness Wildlife

Float with Carl the Wise Old Canoe as he travels the Allagash and learns of the animal antics that his Allagash friends are having. Delight with Oscar "the awkward Osprey" when he falls out of the sky and finds the most unusual thing ever, astound to the chilling "tale" about how two young hunters tumble into trouble during The Attack at Partridge Junction.

ALLAGASH TAILS VOLUME IV

A Wilderness Ranger's Journal:

Rendezvous at Devil's Elbow

There is a special feeling to the Allagash; a sense of adventure, the thrill of getting away from it all!

But in the dark of night there is something else. A shadow lingers, hiding beyond the reach of the lantern's fingers of light.

It remains obscure in the midst of the evergreens and old growth. Among the campfires and s'mores, a bone-chilling draft embraces all. Shivering, we draw our coats tighter to protect against the rawness.

In this mystery adventure, journey with ten-year-old Olivia as her family continues to canoe the world famous Allagash River. In the prequel to the popular An Allagash Haunting, they've only been on the water for four days and already Livy has experienced enough to last a lifetime.

OUTREACH PROGRAMS:

Allagash Tails and Tales

Bring the Maine woods and the stories behind the Allagash Tails Collection of books to your classroom, library, or organization.

In an hour-long multi-media PowerPoint program, author Tim Caverly will present the north woods as you've never seen it before. Learn about the natural and logging history of this nationally significant watershed and/or enjoy a reading from one of our books. We have several PowerPoint programs available; please contact us to receive more information about how you can enjoy a presentation in your community.

Play adaptations of An Allagash Haunting

Watch the characters of Olivia, Jacquelyn, Kevin, and Allie the Golden Retriever come to life in the stage creation and readers' theater versions of the story about family, friends, and our north woods legacy. Contact us at www.allagashtails. com for information on how to bring this production to your community.

Radio Play of An Allagash Haunting

Hear the story as told on Houlton, Maine, radio station WHOU 100.1 FM and performed by the Houlton Starbright Theatre. Listen to the call of the loon; hear the quick tempo of the old-time French Canadian music. Picture in your mind and thrill with the cast of characters as a family takes a trip to the Maine woods, as only the radio can describe.

COMING SOON:

Watch for more animal antics from Maine's premier natural areas and other stories that are classic Maine.

For more information visit our website at

www.AllagashTails.com